RIGHT STUFF
For New
Hang Glider Pilots

Erik Fair

with illustrations by
Rod Stafford and Rick Zimbelman

RIGHT STUFF For New Hang Glider Pilots

by Erik Fair

Published by:

Publitec Editions
271 Lower Cliff Dr.
Post Office Box 4342
Laguna Beach, CA   92652

Library of Congress Cataloging in Publication Data:

Fair, Erik, 1945 -
    Right stuff for new hang glider pilots.

    Includes index.
    1. Hang gliding. I. Title
GV764.F35   1986   7987.5'5   84-60909
ISBN 0-913581-00-3

Foreword

Erik Fair has been flying hang gliders for ten years, and teaching hang gliding for seven. He teaches better than he flies, which suggests to me that aptitude is more important than length of experience. What he does best, however, is write, particularly when he is writing about hang gliding.

You can learn about flying hang gliders from this book. You won't learn about designing them, and you won't learn much about the technical aspects of how they work. There's very little "theory" in the following pages. Instead, there are a lot of observations based on experience; the stuff of which real knowledge is made. Erik's special talent is his ability to distill the essential lessons from these observations and to convey them to the reader in a humorous, accessible, and entertaining style.

Erik is at his best when he is reducing the complex aspects of airmanship to simple, down home homilies that could have come straight off the farm, such as "Never solicit advice from a pilot named 'Crash' or 'Freestyle' who says 'right on,' 'that's cool,' and 'go for it' in the same sentence."

I enjoyed reading this book. I think you will too. Beyond that, there is every probability that you will learn some things that will make you a better pilot.

Mike Meier

Mike Meier

Preface

Hey. How you doin'? Listen up for a minute while I let you in on a few things you'll want to know before diving into this book.

First, if you don't already know, what we have here is a collection of articles all of which appeared in Hang Gliding magazine starting in 1981 and ending in 1986. That means this volume is not to be confused with anything comprehensive or tightly organized. On the other hand, it IS loosely organized around a particular viewpoint — to the extent that a general love of hang gliding, good times, and personal safety can be considered to be a particular viewpoint.

Second, you need to know that the truest statement between these covers is found on page 99. And I quote:

> "The truth is this: My articles are at best useless and at worst dangerous UNLESS they are used in conjunction with or subsequent to completion of a competent training program."

Don't you dare try to use this book as a substitute for a competent training program. If you do it will end in tears for you and an out-thrust lower lip for me. Please, please, PLEASE learn how to hang glide in person from a professional.

What else? There is, if I do say so myself, plenty of useful information and a grin or two to be gleaned from this book. The grins are clean and unencumbered. The information must be evaluated in the context of whatever instructional program you are following. Why? Because every instructional program is a little different, and there are bound to be statements in this book with which your own instructor will disagree — perhaps strongly.

I'm thinking of Joe Greblo's reaction to my assessment of knee hanger harnesses. Joe, whose very successful teaching system utilizes knee hanger harnesses, read the "Going Prone" article and then called me up to politely suggest that my total panning of a piece of equipment he has used successfully for years perhaps indicated a degree of arrogance, even irresponsibility, on my part.

Though Joe is far too short and uppity to be taken too very seriously, I had to consider his point well taken. And so I say this to you: If your instructor disagrees with anything in this book, simply make him explain his own viewpoint in context of his own instructional system and — if he does so to your satisfaction — ignore me very quickly and without question.

Having said all that I'd like to acknowledge a bunch of people whose enormous contributions to hang gliding in general and/or instructional technique in particular have meant a great deal to me throughout my hang gliding career. They are, in no specific order, Ken de Russy, Joe Greblo, Dan Skadal, Rob McKenzie, Greg De Wolf, Rob Kells, Steve Pearson, all members of the loosely formed Hang Glider Dealer's Association, all surviving manufacturers of hang gliders, and most anyone else who has perservered through the years in the always tough and sometimes wonderful business end of hang gliding.

Finally (yes, finally), I must say that every author, whether he admits it or not, has one key person for whom — to whom — he is basically writing. The advice of that person is held in highest regard and the approval of that person is most urgently sought.

For me, since I first started writing about hang gliding, that person has been Michael Meier, whose legendary ugliness is — I swear to God — only skin deep.

Hope y'all have as much fun with this book as I did.

Erik Fair

Erik Fair

Contents

Illustrations

*Dedicated to Alfalfa
and Captain Cool Shoes.*

1. The Parable of R2D2 and MAT

So you've taken a batch of hang gliding lessons, worked hard, learned well, and your reward is expulsion from the security of your instructor's nest. Or, possibly, it's more like you've finally been turned loose by that smothering instructor of yours and you're finally free to develop your hang gliding skills on your own.

Freedom! No more sand in your shoes. No more weeds or seeds in your shorts. No more humping a 60-pound glider up that wretched little 150-foot hill you've trained on for what seems like your last 12 lifetimes. Altitude! Soaring! The big payoff!

Okay, calm down. There are a few things you have to look at. The fact is you may no longer be under direct supervision as you prepare to go about becoming a more skilled and fulfilled pilot. What's more you basically know only two things:

1. Safe hang gliding requires an enormous amount of responsibility and self-discipline.

2. Hang gliding is so outrageously fun and exciting that you are virtually exploding with the desire to do more and get better. Right now!

Let's assume your instructor has carefully installed the Responsibility-Discipline computer (R2D2) in your head. R2D2 is a droll little electronic humanoid not unlike his Star Wars namesake. He represents the evaluative, conservative, data seeking, "process-all-the-variables-before-flying" part of you. He lives in your head where he is more protected from MAT, whom you're about to meet.

Let's also assume that the experience of flight has resulted in a benevolent but out of control thrilla gorilla named MAT (More Air Time!) taking up residence on your back. Furthermore, MAT is grinning insanely, energetically stomping to the tune of "Orange Blossom Special," and threatening to shake poor R2D2 to electro-bits unless you give him all his bananas right now. Bananas to MAT are seconds, minutes, hours of airtime under any and all conditions, wherever and whenever. He gives you boatloads of energy and motivation.

Your dilemma, Novice pilot, is this: You need both these characters to develop into a living Intermediate then Advanced pilot. What makes it tough is that, left to their own devices, R2D2 and MAT will probably refuse to work together. In fact, they routinely plot to kill each other as soon as you're not looking. It is up to you to become a Kissinger-like shuttle diplomat just to keep both these guys alive and on your side.

Quite specifically, your task is to preserve and develop R2D2 because he generally matures more slowly and is most vulnerable to destruction at the Novice level. You simply try to satiate MAT who is generally most powerful at the Novice level. Rest assured, MAT will probably calm down a little bit in two or three years and will definitely get much easier to control as R2D2 grows stronger.

An obscure poet, James Tate, inadvertently suggests how best to deal with MAT during his Novice days. The last lines of "How the Friends Met" are as follows:

So what do you do? What
can you do? Kick him out?
Hell, no. You charge him rent.

In the meantime, do everything you can to accumulate more knowledge to fill up R2D2's vast circuitry. Simultaneously, develop ways to keep MAT under control but still excited.

To help you do this, subsequent articles will address, among other topics:

1. Reliable sources of information for the Novice pilot.

2. Frameworks and/or criteria to help schedule and implement new learning experiences.

3. The role of self-awareness in flying safely.

4. Common traps and pitfalls you can expect to encounter as you play shuttle diplomat to R2D2 and MAT.

2. Information Sources For the New Pilot

This article is intended to outline and discuss the major sources of new information and learning experience for the Novice pilot. Everybody knows that learning to hang glide, like learning to do anything else, is a continuing process of accumulating new information and experience.

Furthermore, the relationship between information and experience is circular. One leads to the other endlessly. For instance, you read about coordinating turns, then go practice coordinated turns, then understand more of what you read about turns, then turn more efficiently next time out. Remember this concept of the cosmic circle of information and experience. It will help you sort through the nonsense as you utilize the resources we're about to examine.

CONTINUED CONTACT WITH A PROFESSIONAL INSTRUCTOR

Continued contact with a carefully selected professional instructor is probably the most reliable source of information/experience available to you. You can tap it in a couple of ways.

Formal Intermediate and Advanced courses, for instance, are available through many schools. What you pay for in these courses is a structured blending of information (ground school stuff) and actual flight experience. In selecting specific Intermediate or Advanced programs, what you should look for is a strong correlation between the stated goals of the program and the information/experience provided to meet these goals.

For example, you wouldn't want to sign up for an Intermediate course which consisted of two full days of someone strapping a radio to your keel and talking you through a few honking thermals. A better value would be an Intermediate course that consisted of two ground schools and one flight experience. The first ground school in a course entitled "Thermaling I" would consist of pertinent information about thermal lift, a review of specific skills necessary to utilize it, and personal goal setting for your flight.

Your first in-flight experience in thermal lift then is focused around carefully coordinated information, skills, and goals. The second ground school would be used to analyze your flight in terms of the information/skills/goals and to set new goals.

The point is, when you look for formal Intermediate-Advanced instruction, look for the best (most correlated) blend of information and experience.

Continued informal contact with an instructor is valuable also. All good schools encourage graduated students to keep in touch and are more than happy to provide information or advice. They are motivated in at least two ways. One, they want to keep your goodwill and business. Two, your flying skill is a reflection of their program and they'll do everything they can to keep you looking good. Don't be afraid to pester your instructor.

CLUBS

Some of us, however, tire quickly of the structure and inherent paternalism of formal instruction. If this sounds like you, another fairly reliable source of information/experience is hang gliding clubs. A club is simply a group of people with common interests and concerns. Club membership will give you regular exposure to a variety of pilots at different levels of experience. You can learn from their successes and mistakes. Every bent downtube, out-landing, or magic flight by some other club member offers you a learning experience.

Clubs also provide for a division of labor in scheduling parachute seminars, arranging for guest speakers, and planning trips to new sites. Clubs, in short, can give R2D2 new data and simulaneously provide a few bananas for MAT who loves to talk about bent downtubes and trips to Big Sur.

OTHER PILOTS

Some of us, however, tire quickly of groups and organizations. If this sounds like you, other lone wolf pilots can be a great source of information/experience. On the other hand, they can be a deadly source.

The problem is you have no idea what the other pilot's background is and he has no idea where you're coming from. MAT gets a golden opportunity to shop around for advice he wants to hear while R2D2 simply "does not compute" due to lack of pertinent data.

Also, experienced pilots, even if well-intentioned, have been known to be a rather self-centered, aloof lot who are so eager to dive into a thermal that they'll tell you anything you want to hear just to shut you up.

One of my students whose real name is Mat (ah, the irony) was the victim of his own ignorance coupled with experienced pilot feedback. An Elsinore local saw Mat land after a sled ride from Edwards Bowl (Hang II stuff) and proclaimed him ready to fly the "E" (Hang IV stuff). In reality, Mat's readiness to fly the "E" corresponded with the local's need to get a ride to the top. Yet another local at the "E," when Mat asked him what to do, told him: "Just follow those other guys; but stay out of our way." Mat crashed, escaped serious injury, and is now more careful about who he listens to.

The point here is be very careful in soliciting advice from pilots you don't know. A good way to approach using this resource is to ask specific questions in areas where you have some knowledge and experience. Questions like "Can I fly here, now?" get low quality answers like "Sure," "What do I care," "No," etc. Questions like "How do you get your 360's so tight and flat?," assuming you're already doing coordinated 360's, may get answers you can use.

A great rule of thumb is:

Never solicit advice from a pilot named "Crash" or "Freestyle" who says "right on," "that's cool," and "go for it" in the same sentence.

CLASSES AND READING MATERIAL

Books, magazines, and classes can provide enormous amounts of good information which you can use to channel your experience. Hang gliding and sailplane publications also provide good information though they are certainly less focused on the needs of the Novice pilot. There are extended hang gliding ground schools in some colleges in some areas. Classes in aviation, aerodynamics, and meteorology are more generally available and provide good background information.

The obvious limitation of written and academic information is they are experience poor. Avoid the subtle trap of over dependence on these sources. You can waste a lot of time learning about thermals if you try to understand your real experience with them strictly in terms of an idealized model thermal described in a book or magazine.

SUMMARY

Experience and information are the keys to your development as a hang glider pilot. Seek them out and use them in tandem. Ideally, you should utilize all the information/experience resources discussed above. Above all, realize that you are the only one who really knows how R2D2 and MAT are maturing inside you. As long as you're giving orders to them and not vice-versa you've got great times ahead as you go and grow as a hang glider pilot.

3. USHGA Pilot Proficiency Rating System

This article is intended to provide the Novice pilot a framework which can be used to schedule and implement new learning experiences. The framework presented is basically a summary of the Pilot Proficiency Rating System enacted by the USHGA Safety and Training Committee. Space and time considerations, as well as my desire to emphasize the rating system as a learning tool, have made it necessary to edit the material slightly.

As a professional instructor I was greatly pleased to find that the general structure and specific content of the rating system make it an ideal training tool. It is set up with specific **required witnessed tasks** and **recommended operating limitations** for each proficiency level. As you progress from beginning to advanced levels the tasks become more exacting (a reflection of your increased skills) and the operating limitations become less restrictive (a reflection of your increased knowledge and experience). Also, the system is up to date! In its organization and progression it deals with today's equipment, knowledge, and training methods. If you read, understand, and follow this system, you will maximize your chances of developing safely as a hang glider pilot.

The first thing the rating system does is require that all participating pilots, no matter what their proficiency level, consistently demonstrate good judgment and maturity. The Safety and Training Committee defines good judgment as: The ability to make decisions, as a pilot, so as never to endanger other people, nor interfere with their rights, nor jeopardize the use of a flying site. They define maturity as: The consistent practice of good judgment. I maintain that the definition of good judgment should include not being a danger to yourself as well.

The Special Skills and USHGA Master Rating will not be discussed in this article. As a point of interest, you should know that the Safety and Training Committee is developing updated oral exams for the Beginner and Novice ratings and updated written exams for the Intermediate and Advanced ratings.

And now, the specifics of the Pilot Proficiency Rating System.

BEGINNER

Required Witnessed Tasks

1. Setup and pre-flight glider and harness.

2. Demonstrates proper ground handling, including familiarity with glider owner's manual.

3. Demonstrates method of confirming hook-in just prior to launch.

4. Unassisted launch with aggressive run, proper angle of attack, directional control, smooth transition from running to flying.

5. Proper airspeed recognition and smooth control of airspeed well above stall.

6. Safe, smooth landing on feet into the wind.

7. Shows ability to recognize and understand effect of varying wind conditions at training site.

8. Demonstrates understanding of proper breakdown, packing, transportation, and storing of glider.

Recommended Operating Limitations

1. Fly only in winds of 12 mph or less with gust differential of 5 mph or less.

2. Launch only on slopes of 3-1 to 6-1 where wind is within 15 degrees of straight up slope.

3. Launch only where there are no obstructions within 60 degrees to either side of intended flight path and when pilot may fly straight from launch to landing with no need to maneuver and no possibility of out-flying landing area.

4. Should maintain flight heading within 15 degrees of straight into the wind.

5. Should fly appropriate sites so as to maintain altitude below 100' AGL.

6. Should exceed these limitations only after thoroughly mastering all required tasks and after acquiring a full understanding of the potential problems and dangers involved in exceeding these limitations.

NOTE: Pay special attention to operating limitation 6. It forces you to anticipate the dangers involved in progressing as much as you anticipate the rewards.

NOVICE

Required Witnessed Tasks (in addition to Beginner requirements)

1. Successful, aggressive, confident launches on a slope shallower than 4-1 with less than 6 mph wind. Can launch where wind is crossing 15 degrees from straight uphill in winds not exceeding 5 mph.

2. Demonstrates flights along a planned path with alternating "S" turns of at least 90 degrees change in heading. Flight heading not to exceed 45 degrees from straight into wind. Turns must be smooth with controlled airspeed.

3. Demonstrates 3 consecutive landings within 100' of a target. Landings must be safe, smooth, on feet, and into wind. Target must be sufficiently close to launch that turns are required to set up approach and must be at least 100' below launch point.

4. Demonstrates flights with smooth variation in airspeed between minimum sink speed and fast flight. Should not mush or stall glider at any time. Should approach minimum sink speed only in smooth conditions with at least 75' ground clearance.

Operating Limitations

1. Fly only in smooth winds of 18 mph or less. Gusty winds of 11 mph or less.

2. Launch only on slopes of 2-1 to 7-1 where wind is within 25 degrees of straight up slope.

3. Maintain flight heading within 90 degrees of directly into wind, and within 45 degrees of directly into wind below 60' AGL.

4. Should not attempt to fly slowly (minimum sink) when encountering lift but instead concentrate on maintaining altitude, heading, and airspeed.

5. Should exeed these limitations only after thoroughly mastering all required tasks and after acquiring a full understanding of the potential problems and dangers involved in exceeding these limitations.

NOTE: The Safety and Training Committee strongly recommends that all Beginner and Novice flights be made under the direct supervision of a USHGA certified basic or advanced instructor, or observer.

INTERMEDIATE

Requirements

1. Novice rating for 4 months.

2. At least 30 logged flying days, 90 logged flights, and 2 hours logged air time.

Required Witnessed Tasks (in addition to Beginner and Novice tasks)

1. Has received and understands the importance and significance of:

   a. Right of way rules.
   b. FAA regulations and sectionals.
   c. Airspeed control, stalls, spins, adverse yaw.
   d. Glider owner's manual.
   e. USHGA accident report results currently in print.

2. Can give verbal analysis of conditions on the hill demonstrating knowledge of wind shadows, gradient, lift, sink, laminar air, turbulence, and rotors, and the effects of these on intended flight paths and turns.

3. Can give verbal flight plan for each observed flight.

4. Differentiates between airspeed and ground speed.

5. Demonstrates linked 180-degree turns along a predetermined ground track showing smooth controlled reversals and proper coordination at various speeds and bank angles.

6. Explains stall warning characteristics.

7. Has practiced and demonstrates gentle stalls and proper recovery under the direct supervision of an instructor or observer, at least 500' from any object.

8. In 8-15 mph wind demonstrates ability to maintain airspeed at or near minimum sink. No evidence of stall during crosswind and upwind legs.

9. Demonstrates 3 consecutive spot landings within 50' of a target after flights requiring approach turns.

10. Demonstrates proper airspeed control when descending through a gradient.

11. Demonstrates proper airspeed control for maximum distance flown into a significant headwind.

Recommended Operating Limitations

1. Fly only in winds of 25 mph or less with gust differential of 10 mph or less.

2. Initiate downwind turns only with 500' clearance outward from terrain in winds between 10 and 18 mph.

3. Upon mastering the above skills, the Intermediate pilot should pursue new maneuvers, sites, and conditons with the guidance of a USHGA certified advanced instructor or observer.

ADVANCED

Requirements

1. Intermediate rating for at least 8 months.

2. Logged at least 250 flights, 5 flights at each of 5 level III sites (at least 3 inland), 80 flying days, one 60-minute flight, one 30-minute flight in thermal lift without sustaining ridge lift, 50 hours airtime.

Required Witnessed Tasks (in addition to Beginner, Novice, Intermediate tasks)

1. Demonstrates ability to allow for clearance and drift when doing 360-degree turns. Does so by doing 2 consecutive coordinated figure 8's in a wind sufficient to cause drift.

2. Demonstrates 3 consecutive spot landings within 25' of a target.

3. Demonstrates smooth, coordinated 360-degree turns in both directions, with reversals at various speeds and bank angles.

4. Demonstrates intentional stalls straight ahead and in turns showing smooth, confident recoveries. Ground clearance of at least 500' AGL.

5. Demonstrates ability to soar above a low point for 5 minutes on each of 3 different flights.

6. Demonstrates an altitude gain of at least 500' in thermals.

Recommended Operating Limitation

Should not fly within 30' of another glider in smooth air or 100' of another glider in moderately turbulent air.

4. Launch Considerations: Angle of Attack

I have witnessed a number of launches lately that have led me to the conclusion that it is high time to reiterate (repeat loudly — in no uncertain terms) the relationship between angle of attack and airspeed in the context of launch technique. It is our mutual good fortune that this is a subject area that can best be explored and explained through the use of Rod Stafford's eye pleasing illustrations with a minimum of guff from yours truly.

For instance, look at Figure 1. It clearly shows what angle of attack is.

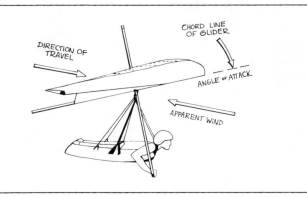

Figure 1. What angle of attack is.

All I get to do is tell you what you already know which is that life giving airspeed varies inversely with angle of attack. The more you got of one, the less you got of the other and vice versa.

Perhaps a little jingle will nail this concept down for all of us:

Lower the nose, blow off your clothes
Raise the angle, helplessly dangle

Ho Hum. Let's go to Figure 2 on the next page so we can wake up.

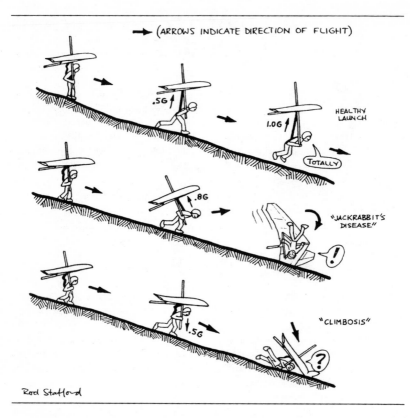

Figure 2. Launch sequences.

Any set of illustrations which features two blown launches and only one good one is at least as stimulating as a cup of coffee.

Before we discuss the three launch sequences shown you gotta know this: Beyond the ability to properly judge conditions vis-a-vis your own capabilities, there are only two secrets to good launch technique. Not surprisingly, both have to do with angle of attack. Secret One: Position your glider wings level and stationary (neither rolling nor yawing) at the "proper" angle of attack BEFORE you initiate your takeoff run. Secret Two: Maintain "proper" angle of attack throughout your takeoff run which you will enthusiastically continue until such time as your entire weight is smoothly transitioned onto the glider.

What constitutes "proper" angle of attack? That can vary somewhat with conditions, shape of the launch area, and the static balance of the glider you're using. For the purposes of discussion, just so's we can isolate a few key variables, we're going to declare a smooth, straight-in 5 mph wind, at a smooth 5 to 1 launch area, in a perfectly statically balanced fixed airfoil glider. As illustrated in Figure 2, the proper initial angle of attack in this case is "slightly" above neutral so that the glider will begin to support its own weight as soon as the pilot initiates his run.

The first sequence shows a pilot initiating and completing his launch without changing his angle of attack. He had it right to begin with (approximately trim bar position) and did not have to adjust to gusts so he simply ran until the glider developed enough airspeed to lift him away from the slope. How much airspeed was enough? At the angle of attack that corresponds to trim bar position in this example, about 20 mph. Note that as he progresses from the set position (AS = WS = 5 mph) to lift off (AS = 20 mph) the glider supports a smoothly increasing percentage of his weight. This is as it should be.

The second sequence shows a pilot performing what we in the trade call a "Jack Rabbit" start. The problem with sprinter's block starts in mild conditions is that the pilot literally fails to bring the not-as-yet flying glider with him in his first few steps. Since the statically balanced glider is no longer supported by the pilot's shoulders (which are now thrust through the control bar) it quite naturally falls back thereby raising the angle of attack dramatically. Maybe the pilot will be able to "tug" the glider back to a runable angle of attack once his harness straps go tight but more often than not he won't get it back.

What will happen is one of two things: The glider will leave the ground at an airspeed commensurate with the "too high" angle of attack (say 12 mph). The pilot will lose directional control of the slow moving glider and spin off to the side. Sometimes both happen. Obviously, neither way is any good. Avoid this problem by making sure you "bring the glider with you" on your first few steps. After that it will be flying (supporting its own weight) and will seek to keep your initial angle of attack, in this case, trim.

If you suspect you are having this problem in light wind takeoffs there is a way to find out for sure without putting yourself at risk. Use Dan Skadal's technique which has been proven on hundreds of students. Ground run your glider on nearly flat ground in light or no wind without using a harness. If you have "Jack Rabbit's" disease the symptoms will appear in the form of your glider falling behind you as you try to sprint forward. Because you are not in a harness you won't be able to "tug" the glider back into proper position as you may be in the habit of doing. (You listenin', Leroy?)

Here's the remedy: Use your shoulders to support the weight of the glider as you smoothly initiate your run. When you feel the glider lift off your shoulders and support its own weight you are in a position to accelerate your run, assuming the angle of attack is the same as when you started. This problem generally does not appear in winds over 8 mph because that's about what it takes to support the weight of a modern glider at a trim angle of attack.

The third sequence in Figure 2 shows the opposite problem. Here the pilot allows the glider to end up ahead of him without his weight being applied to the CG (note slack harness straps). More often than not this sequence begins with a hesitant, pitty pat run followed by the pilot trying to "climb" into the control bar. The act of supporting weight on the control bar not only reduces the pilot's mobility and fluidity but, more importantly, applies weight well in front of the CG, thereby lowering the angle of attack and putting the glider further in front of the pilot who must then "chase" even faster after it. No fun here at all!! Note that as the sequence continues the pilot appears to be pushing out more and more in an attempt to save the launch. Of course he's not REALLY pushing out as far as the glider is concerned because there ain't nobody attached to the CG, just some fool chasing along with a little weight on the control bar.

If this problem sounds suspiciously familiar to you, do ground runs in light wind with your harness on. Smear Vaseline all over them downtubes so you can't support weight on 'em and run until you look and feel like the pilot in the first sequence. (You can skip the Vaseline if you promise not to "climb." After all, there is your reputation to think of.)

Figure 3, opposite, has nothing to do with angle of attack but it DOES have something to do with a very important aspect of launch so I invited it to appear for your consideration. What we have here is an imprecise illustration of the relationship between percentage of pilot weight being carried by the glider and the amount of pilot motion required to effect a given directional correction.

Note that until your glider is carrying a fair percentage of your weight (say 25%) you are essentially without aerodynamic roll/yaw control. Between 0 and 25% you are basically dependent on physical manipulation (muscling, pulling, shouldering, grunting) to keep the glider straight and level. Therefore it's a real good idea to make sure you start your run only when the glider is SET (not yawing or rolling around). It's very difficult at best to get a modern glider back into shape if you start your run "out of shape."

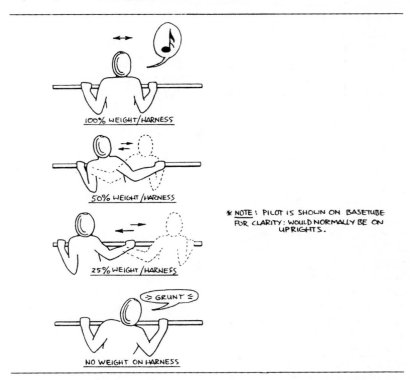

Figure 3. Weight on glider vs. motion needed for correction.

Note further that at 25% you need the whole bar to make a moderate corrective turn through weight shift and that only after 100% of your weight is in the glider will it respond to weight shift in the manner you know best.

For all you literalists and technicians out there let me hasten to admit that the illustrated percentages and distances were not scientifically computed. They were "computed" via the "squinted eye, out thrust tongue and thumb" methodology I'm most comfortable with. Plus I asked Mike (Who You Callin' Ugly) Meier what HE thought and HE SCRATCHED HIS HEAD APPROVINGLY before throwing me out of his office. Anyway, it's the principle that needed illustrating.

Figure 4 illustrates how a change in the direction of the airflow can effect a change in angle of attack, therefore airspeed.

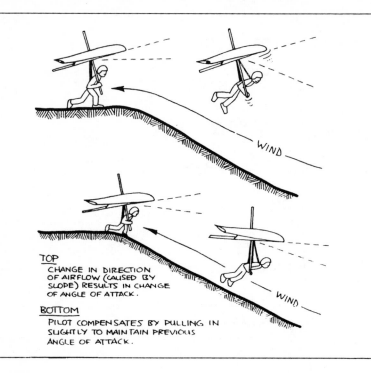

Figure 4. Effect of airflow change on angle of attack.

Note that in the first sequence of Figure 4 the attitude of the glider remains the same but the angle of attack is raised by the change in direction of the airflow at the point where the pilot reaches the slope. To maintain the same angle of attack throughout the take-off run the pilot must anticipate the change in the airflow and pull in slightly to compensate. Actually, in a vast majority of cases, the better option is to START the takeoff run right where the slope begins. No guess, no mess.

Figure 5, following, represents an extreme example of the point discussed under Figure 4. Some high wind cliff launch situations call for the seemingly radical "nose down" positioning of the glider on the launch ramp. Note the angle of attack as illustrated. Imagine what the angle of attack would be in a more "normal looking" positioning of the glider. Gives one pause, no?

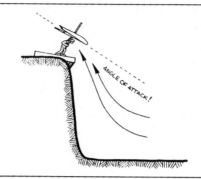

Figure 5. Angle of attack, high wind cliff launch.

I am compelled to note that true blue high wind launches can be extremely deceptive (look easy, are dangerous). Never do one cold turkey. Observe, discuss, and understand each one on an individual basis.

SUMMARY

Having reneged on my promise to let the pictures tell the story I will conclude with an incredibly concise and pertinent "merry little ditty":

> *Runnin' fast with flamin' feet*
> *Is, no doubt, neat,*
> *Pete.*
>
> *But don't forget (It's a natchel' fact)*
> *You gotta maintain yo' angle of attack,*
> *Jack.*

HEY!! WAKE UP! HAVE A CUPPA COFFEE OR SOMETHIN' !!!

5. How to Land a Flex Wing

The preceding article has given you the best information available on how to maintain proper angle of attack while launching. The launch is probably the single most critical aspect of hang glider flight because during launch you and your glider are close to the ground, flying only slightly above stall speed.

Well folks, there is yet another single most critical aspect of hang glider flight that occurs close to the ground and slightly above stall speed. "How to Land a Flex Wing" is the subject of this article. More specifically, we're going to examine the landing sequence from completion of your final approach turn to touchdown. We're going to ask and answer the question: Why is landing so demanding? Then, we're going to recommend a specific technique to bring you from final to mother earth as gracefully as a bird lands in a tree.

WHY LANDING IS DEMANDING

The goal of landing a hang glider is simple enough: To touch suitable ground, gently, feet first, wings level, at 0 mph ground speed at a place that is reasonably close to where you want to be.

The list of variables you have to consider in landing a hang glider is basic enough: wind speed and direction, wind gradient, airspeed, ground speed, ground effect, recognition and avoidance of obstacles, and execution of corrective turns.

Why then am I trying to tell you that bringing a hang glider in from final to touchdown is a demanding task? I'll put it simply: Landing a hang glider is not something you can do exactly when you want to. You can pick the exact moment you start your takeoff run, but you cannot pick the exact moment you land. Once you're on final approach you are committed to reacting immediately and appropriately to whatever comes your way in regard to changing conditions, sudden appearance of obstacles, etc.

Since it is more difficult for you as a relatively inexperienced pilot to react immediately and appropriately, it is especially important for you to go to the landing area before each flight to check out conditions and to make sure a highly visible flag is present. If you discover that the landing area is swirling with dust devils or that the flag is switching 90 degrees every five minutes, DON'T FLY even if conditions at launch are perfect. One more time: You DO NOT get to choose the exact conditions you're going to land in. Make sure the odds are they'll be conditions you can handle.

CALM AIR LANDING

So your best judgment tells you the odds are excellent that you can deal effectively with conditions in the landing area. You take off, fly around happily for as long as conditions permit, then decide it's time to deal with landing. You notice that the flag in the LZ is motionless and set up for final approach with a dead air landing in mind. Figure 6 shows two pilots (Right Stuff and Wrong Stuff) setting up for final approach.

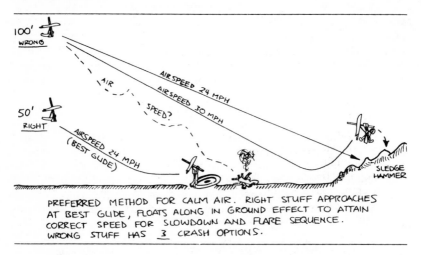

PREFERRED METHOD FOR CALM AIR. RIGHT STUFF APPROACHES AT BEST GLIDE, FLOATS ALONG IN GROUND EFFECT TO ATTAIN CORRECT SPEED FOR SLOWDOWN AND FLARE SEQUENCE. WRONG STUFF HAS <u>3</u> CRASH OPTIONS.

Figure 6. Suggested final landing approach, calm air.

In Figure 6, Right Stuff approaches at best glide. At 4' from the ground he enters ground effect which flattens his glide path. At this point he begins his slowdown/flare sequence. Wrong Stuff has 3 crash options.

Notice first that Right Stuff has set up for final at the proper altitude. His glider performs at an 8-1 best glide ratio. The target is 400' away and his altitude is 50' (8 x 50' = 400'). Upon completion of his final approach turn Right Stuff swings into landing position, legs down, hands transitioned to the downtubes of his control bar. His eyes are focused on the target. He is pulling in slightly on the bar so that his airspeed is about at best glide, 24 IAS (indicated airspeed). Note that his glide path at 24 mph IAS intersects the ground slightly before the bullseye. Not to worry. Right Stuff knows that approximately 4' from the ground he will enter ground effect and his glide path will flatten somewhat. He cruises in ground effect, timing small 1-2" push-outs with the goal of maintaining about 3' ground clearance. When he feels and hears that the glider is stalling he dramatically pushes the control bar out and up thereby bringing it to a complete stop.

Let's isolate and explain everything Right Stuff did in his dead air landing:

1. Final approach turn at approximately correct altitude: Minimizes chances of over- and under-shooting target.

2. In landing position throughout final approach: Extra body drag lowers the L/D ratio and steepens the approach. The steeper one's glide on approach, the less one's point of landing is affected by errors or changes in altitude. Hands always in contact with bar: can react immediately.

3. Hands on downtubes: Better fulcrum for complete flare.

4. Eyes focused on target: You tend to land where you look.

5. Approach at best glide speed: Maximum controllability of glider during approach. Ability to adjust glide path by either speeding up OR slowing down slightly.

6. Relying on ground effect: The glide path of any glider ALWAYS flattens somewhat as in comes within 4-5' of the ground. This is because the ground reduces induced drag by blocking formation of extended wingtip vortices.

7. Gradual slowdown to stall speed maintaining 3' ground clearance: Avoids "flying into ground" or slowing down too suddenly which results in climb out, stall, stall-break, and pound.

8. Dramatic flare as stall speed is reached: Fully stops glider in relation to ground. Too late a flare is equivalent to throwing glider in front of you as there is insufficient lift to stop glider. Incomplete or "take it back" flare results in continued forward momentum of glider.

Now let's see how Wrong Stuff is making out after setting up his final approach way too high. If he does everything else right he'll fly into the rocks. Wrong Stuff isn't an idiot — he won't do that. What he'll usually do in this situation is slow down to right around stall and mush on in, barely in control of the glider and without ability to flare (he's already pushed out!). At best he'll land on the bull mushing vertically at a speed equivalent to that achieved by jumping off the top of a van. At worst his glider will stall-break 30' off the ground and he'll center punch the bull with his nose plate. If he takes the fast route (30 AS) he'll have a great view of the rocks just before he crashes into them. Let's give Wrong Stuff some credit and save him from crashing by allowing him to S-turn through his approach so he can land between the bull and the rocks.

LANDING INTO A SMOOTH HEADWIND

Look at Figure 7.

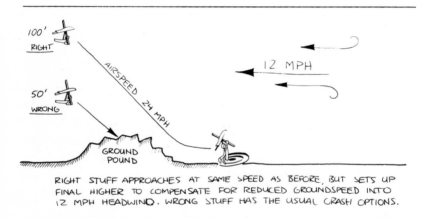

RIGHT STUFF APPROACHES AT SAME SPEED AS BEFORE, BUT SETS UP FINAL HIGHER TO COMPENSATE FOR REDUCED GROUNDSPEED INTO 12 MPH HEADWIND. WRONG STUFF HAS THE USUAL CRASH OPTIONS.

Figure 7. Suggested final landing approach, 12 mph wind.

In this figure, Right Stuff approaches at the same speed as before but sets up his final approach higher to compensate for reduced ground speed into a 12 mph headwind. Wrong Stuff has the same crash options as in Figure 6 (2 shown).

Right Stuff again sets up final at the proper altitude. Note his glide path is twice as steep this time because he's flying into a 12 mph headwind which cuts his ground speed in half. Almost everything else is the same for Right Stuff as it was in his dead air landing. Most notably his approach speed remains at best glide. The only difference is that his experience of being in ground effect will occur over a shorter horizontal distance and his final flare will not have to be as dramatic because he can achieve 0 mph ground speed at touchdown with 12 mph airspeed — the equivalent of the wind velocity. Wrong Stuff, after his experience in dead air, decides to set up final approach lower. Too low, in fact. He can either fly into the rocks at best glide or faster or he can mush into the trees at somewhere between minimum sink and stall. Poor fellow can't S-turn out of this one.

THE EFFECT OF WIND GRADIENT

Figure 8 shows Right and Wrong descending through a wind gradient on final approach.

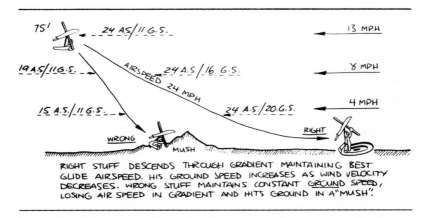

RIGHT STUFF DESCENDS THROUGH GRADIENT MAINTAINING BEST GLIDE AIRSPEED. HIS GROUND SPEED INCREASES AS WIND VELOCITY DECREASES. WRONG STUFF MAINTAINS CONSTANT GROUND SPEED, LOSING AIR SPEED IN GRADIENT AND HITS GROUND IN A "MUSH".

Figure 8. Effect of wind gradient on final approach.

Here, Right Stuff descends through the gradient maintaining constant 24 mph AS. His ground speed gradually increases as the wind velocity decreases. Entering ground effect 4' off the ground, he begins the slowdown/flare sequence. Wrong Stuff maintains constant ground speed on final, gradually losing airspeed and hits the ground in the mushing portion of a stall with insufficient airspeed to flare.

Note that Right Stuff maintains his airspeed at best glide speed throughout his final approach. He experiences a gradual increase in ground speed as he descends through the wind gradient. But Right Stuff is cool. He is able to judge his airspeed and confirm its constancy at best glide by listening, feeling, and seeing what's going on around him.

Wrong Stuff figures he's starting to fly too fast as he descends through the gradient. He figures this because his ground speed is increasing. So Wrong Stuff pushes out and stalls into the ground short of his target. This guy is getting worse!

THE EFFECT OF THERMALS AND/OR GUSTS

Figure 9 shows Right and Wrong encountering a thermal on final approach.

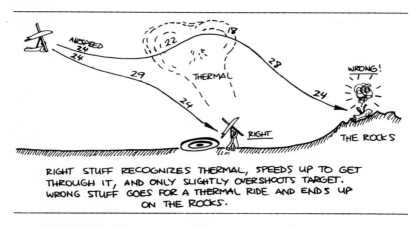

RIGHT STUFF RECOGNIZES THERMAL, SPEEDS UP TO GET THROUGH IT, AND ONLY SLIGHTLY OVERSHOOTS TARGET. WRONG STUFF GOES FOR A THERMAL RIDE AND ENDS UP ON THE ROCKS.

Figure 9. Effect of thermals on final approach.

In this figure, Right Stuff recognizes the thermal, speeds up to get through it, and only slightly overshoots the target. Wrong Stuff goes for a thermal ride and ends up on the rocks. Note that Right counteracts the effect of the thermal by speeding up enough to fly through it. He knows he's on final and is therefore too low to play in thermals. Wrong lets the thermal slow him down to stall speed, his glider stall-breaks, and he's out of control, as usual. The point is, when encountering thermals or gusts on final, by all means speed up. DO NOT slow down or allow yourself to be slowed down.

SUMMARY

You can't land exactly when you want to. From final approach to touchdown you must react immediately and appropriately to changing conditions. Ground effect and, to a lesser extent, wind gradient can be pretty much counted on to affect your approach. Headwinds, thermals, gusts, switches, and kids in the landing area must be experienced and dealt with as they occur.

Look at it this way: There are two things you can control once you're on final approach. You can and must keep yourself pointed into the wind. (In dead air point yourself in the direction the wind usually comes from.) You can and must maintain SUFFICIENT AIRSPEED from final to 4' ground clearance where you begin your slowdown/flare sequence. In calm to moderate conditions sufficient airspeed is best glide. The stronger conditions become, the faster your approach speed should be.

If, following this advice, you find yourself on final approach, bar to the knees with 0 mph ground speed and heading for the rocks, don't blame me. It only means you're trying to land into a 40 mph headwind and that can only mean you didn't read the first part of this article which clearly states: Don't take off into conditions you're not good enough to land in.

6. How to Land a Double Surface, Fixed Airfoil Glider

EEEEEYAAAARGH! (Tippity, tippity, stumble, lunge) SKABAM (Gawww -- dammit!).

How many times have you seen or heard someone land their double surface, fixed airfoil ground slammer in just such a fashion? How many times have you done it yourself? Never mind. I already know.

When I read a letter to the editor from Name Illegible of Tucson, Arizona I instantly realized it was high time someone put an end to the Downtube Derby (or Beakstakes if you will) that has accompanied the advent of fast, efficient gliders that want to keep flying and refuse to land gracefully unless absolutely forced to by proper landing technique. (In case you missed it, Name wrote to Hang Gliding magazine asking for some word on the subject of landing double surface gliders.)

BAD NEWS - GOOD NEWS

The bad news is: Appearances are not deceiving. Double surface, fixed airfoil gliders (DSFAs) really are more difficult to land than the billow cruisers of yesteryear, especially in calm air. Concentration and precise, smooth execution of a specific landing technique are required to bring DSFAs in successfully. There is very little room for error in timing, quantitative inaccuracy in control input, or passive indecision. You have to know what you're doing and be able to do it.

The good news is: All you have to do is finish reading this article and you will know WHY DSFAs are more difficult to land than their ancestors, WHAT you're trying to accomplish during final approach and landing flare, WHICH common errors in technique lead to which kinds of crashes, and HOW to land your DSFA without looking like you're taking a final exam in a survival course. Another bit of good news is that DSFAs are not that hard to land in any significant headwind.

WHY

DSFAs are difficult to land because they are faster and perform better than the gliders they've obsoleted. Now before you leap to the conclusion that Erik Fair has become the champion of the obvious, give me a chance to elaborate.

Faster. You're right, that's easy. Faster means harder to land because your stall speed is higher and that means you can't slow down as much prior to flaring. It also means you have to make the decision to flare when the glider is moving relatively quickly over the ground.

The fact that many pilots avoid making this decision until they are well below stall speed is responsible for a good percentage of pounded DSFA landings. A significant headwind, of course, negates the speed factor and makes DSFAs relatively easy to land.

Higher Performance. Let's define performance as L/D or lift to drag ratio. Let's also grant me a little poetic license so I can simply say that the designers of DSFAs didn't so much spray more L on the wing (though they did a little of that) as they sanded lots of D off the wing. When you spray a little L on and sand lots of D off you have a higher L/D ratio and a better performing hang glider.

Figure 10, opposite, summarizes performance variables of DSFAs and older gliders (billow cruisers) as they pertain to landing issues.

Billow Cruisers	DSFAs
More twist: More drag at stall, more directionally stable.	**Less twist:** Less drag at stall, less directionally stable.
More area: More drag chute effect with flare. (Fully flared glider acts as drag chute.)	**Less area:** Less drag chute effect with flare.
More roll authority: Easier to keep straight and level during slow-down sequence (final approach).	**Less roll authority:** More difficult to keep straight and level during slow-down sequence.
Less pitch sensitivity: Less subject to over-control in pitch.	**More pitch sensitivity:** More subject to over-control in pitch.
Less speed: Slow-down sequence easier and less critical.	**More speed:** Slow-down sequence faster and more critical.
Apparently less increase in L/D due to ground effect: Less time on final spent within a few feet of the ground on landing approach.	**Apparently more increase in L/D due to ground effect:** More time spent within a few feet of the ground on landing approach.

Figure 10. Performance variables: DSFAs, billow cruisers.

Figure 11, following, shows the difference in twist and area between billow cruisers and DSFAs and the concomitant difference in aerodynamic drag at stall speed after flare.

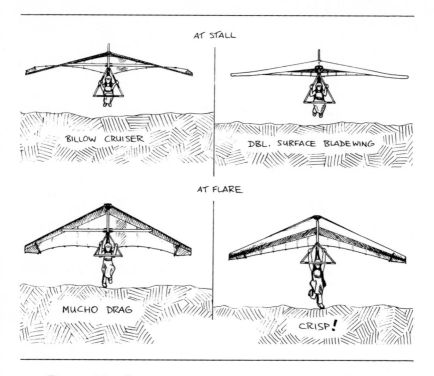

Figure 11. Twist, area comparison: billow cruisers, DSFAs.

WHAT?

What we're talking about here, of course, is landing, the goal of which is to gently touch down on suitable ground at or close to 0 mph ground speed, wings level, on your feet, into the wind, reasonably close to where you want to be. For our purposes landing consists of two parts: **final approach** during which the pilot slows the glider down to stall speed and **flare** which is the process by which the pilot rapidly raises the angle of attack as much as possible, thereby producing maximum drag to bring the glider to a complete stop in relation to the ground.

Since DSFAs SEEM to glide forever once they enter ground effect, and since the landing technique I'm going to recommend to you is based on trying to achieve an infinite glide path at 3' AGL, you can conceive of your entire final approach as occurring at 3' AGL. Further, you can equate drag (D) with what slows you down and lift (L) with what supports your weight (W) while you're slowing down; see Figure 12.

Figure 12. Forces involved in final approach.

We all know you can't glide forever at 3' AGL even in a DSFA glider but if you fly down to 3' AGL at best glide speed and maintain 3' AGL as you gradually slow down to stall speed you will be at 3' AGL for a lot longer time than you would be in an older glider. The sequence is as follows.

1. The goal of final approach is to slow down as much as possible while still flying 3' AGL.

2. As you slow down aerodynamic forces (lift) decrease.

3. You can, up to a point, replace the lift lost to slowing down by increasing your angle of attack.

4. The point at which you can no longer increase lift by raising the angle of attack is stall speed.

5. What you want to do when you reach stall speed and can no longer produce more LIFT by pushing out further is to create as much DRAG as possible as quickly as possible.

6. You do this by executing a complete, aggressive flare.

7. This enables you to land gracefully.

WHICH?

Figure 13 shows three different executions of the 3' above the ground final approach - flare sequence.

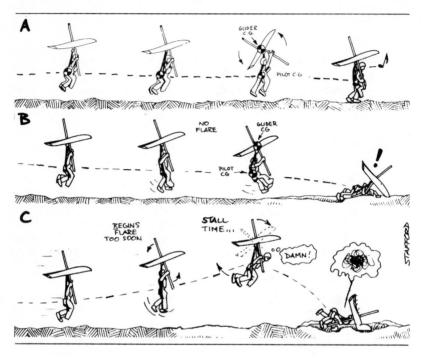

Figure 13. Final approach, flare sequence, 3' AGL.

The first execution (A) is proper. The pilot flies to 3' AGL at best glide, gradually slows down to stall maintaining 3' AGL, then flares at stall speed. He is ready to run so that he can run in front of the glider's static CG. His arms are fully extended above his head as this is the best way to get a complete flare and keep the static CG behind him, so the dead weight of the glider will fall behind him rather than in front of him.

Figure 13-B shows a pilot who has stalled the glider, waited too long, and is therefore unable to flare properly. He has slowed down so much that flaring, instead of utilizing the last bit of usable airspeed to lift the weight of the glider and pilot to a stop has simply thrown the glider in front of him forcing him to run after it. Also the static CG is in front of him and the dead weight of the glider is trying to fall forward. An awkward stumbling nose-in generally results.

Figure 13-C shows a pilot flaring slightly prematurely (before stall speed was reached) and the glider climbing out to 10' AGL. He makes the situation worse by pulling back in. This causes the glider to enter a stall recovery dive which will intersect the ground at a high rate of speed. A better option for a pilot who has flared slightly prematurely and climbed out to as much as 15' is to hold the flare fiercely and land on the keel with the ability to use his legs as shock absorbers. Unnecessary "take it back" flares are responsible for a lot of pounded DSFA landings.

HOW?

Land DSFAs like you land any other glider, only concentrate more and set up as long and straight a final approach as you possibly can.

1. Fly to within 3' AGL at best glide.

2. Maintain 3' AGL while you slow down to stall speed by making small pitch adjustments outward between best glide and 3-4" out from trim bar position.

3. Recognize stall speed by recognizing the point at which you can no longer maintain 3' AGL by pushing out 1". You can develop the ability to feel the point at which the glider stops flying and starts mushing in ground effect.

SUMMARY

1. DSFAs are more difficult to land than billow cruisers because they are faster and perform better in terms of L/D. Faster means you can't slow them down as much during final approach (before you have to flare). Less drag means that when you have slowed them as much as you can and still be flying (stall speed) there is less aerodynamic drag working to destroy your glide path and allow you to land. Less sail area means than the process of flaring does not produce as much drag chute effect. All of the above, coupled with the fact that DSFAs are less roll sensitive and more pitch sensitive makes them noticeably harder to land. There is less room for error in the slowdown and flare sequence.

2. DSFAs can be landed quite gracefully by those who take the time and effort to master proper technique, which consists of slowing down from best glide to stall speed while maintaining 3' AGL, and flaring completely and aggressively at that point. Stay ready to run out of the landing in case you've flared a little bit late. Be convinced that the best thing to do if you've flared a LITTLE early is to hold the flare fiercely and land on the keel, using your legs as shock absorbers.

3. Quit buying downtubes and noseplates.

7. Launch and Landing Problems

Since the last few articles have dealt with takeoff and landing techniques, I thought it would make sense to follow up with an examination of some of the problems Novice pilots commonly experience in the execution of launches and landings.

I have chosen to consider launches and landings together because I have come to believe that the same sorts of behavior that cause blown launches also cause blown landings. I have identified five general problem areas which seem to account for a high percentage of the specific problems I see inexperienced pilots encountering as they run off a hill or cruise into a landing area:

1. Problems related to tension and anxiety.

2. Problems related to airspeed recognition and control.

3. Problems related to body position awareness.

4. Problems related to concentration and focusing.

5. Problems related to judgment of conditions.

Let's take a closer look at each one.

PROBLEMS RELATED TO TENSION AND ANXIETY

At the Beginner and Novice levels a certain amount of tension is unavoidable and a certain amount of anxiety is downright useful. These two brothers tend to work together, however, and if they manage to gain control of your mind and body you can expect to encounter some of the following problems:

Off level takeoffs and landings are the most frequent result of excessive tension and anxiety — what you tend to do in a hang glider when you're tense is to literally hang onto the control bar. Odds are you're stronger on one side than on the other so what you tend to do, even if your body is centered on the control bar, is pull the glider down on one side and put it into a turn. What's worse, any weight you put on the control bar is taken away from the center of gravity and is therefore unavailable to be shifted around to execute corrective turns. If you find yourself getting into surprise turns at takeoff or on final approach, and if you find it really hard to execute corrective turns, odds are you're supporting some weight on the control bar.

Too slow takeoffs and landings. This phenomenon is most dramatically expressed in the well-known "freeze out" maneuver where the pilot goes glassy in the eyes (immobilized by anxiety), locks his arms straight out, and catatonically awaits whatever fate has in store for him. Fortunately, very few pilots "freeze out" and those who do either never do it again or take up bowling.

The bottom line here is that too much anxiety can ruin your ability to think clearly and too much tension can make it impossible to execute proper takeoff and landing technique. If you think you're having tension-anxiety problems try visualizing your body as a pendulum swinging around inside a triangle. Your arms are simply spaghetti-like tentacles to attach to the triangle to give you leverage to shift your weight around. Also, during the week go around daydreaming images of yourself emerging into the sky at takeoff or alighting gracefully in the LZ. Relax.

PROBLEMS RELATED TO
AIRSPEED RECOGNITION AND CONTROL

As we've discovered in the last two articles, if you aren't proficient at recognizing and manipulating airspeed, you're going to have big problems launching and landing a hang glider.

Probably the most common error at launch is what I call **arbitrary runoff.** If most of your limited experience tells you that you can get off in four steps and you try to do that in dead air or on a shallow slope, you are doomed to take off either too slowly or not at all. If you insist on getting your arbitrary four steps into a 20 mph headwind and down a steep slope, you're going to take off too fast or have a greater chance of over-controlling the glider.

If you are **nosing in** or **stalling** takeoffs it means you either don't understand the effect of angle of attack on takeoff or you don't know how to control it. The cure here is to go back to the training hill until you've got it wired.

Probably the most common error in landing is what I call **ground referencing,** or judging your airspeed by how fast the ground is going by. Two things conspire to make many Novice pilots get too slow too soon on landing. First, the closer you get to the ground the faster it <u>appears</u> to be going by. Second, as you descend through the

---

wind gradient your ground speed actually will increase if you maintain constant airspeed — which you should.

If you think your approaches are fine except for the fact that the glider gets really sluggish about 20 feet off the ground, or if you tend to land fully pushed out with lots of vertical speed or forward momentum, you are probably guilty of ground referencing.

Avoid **arbitrary runoff** and **ground referencing** by tuning into the real sound and feel of airspeed. Generally speaking, your feet shouldn't leave the ground until you hear proper airspeed and the glider feels under control and responsive. For landing, remember to fly to within four feet of the ground at best glide speed or above (depending on conditions) before you start your slowdown-flare sequence.

PROBLEMS RELATED TO
POOR BODY AWARENESS

This problem area is characterized by either lack of awareness as to where your weight is or lack of discipline in distributing it. If you're not hanging onto the control bar as discussed earlier and you still get into surprise turns at takeoff or on final approach, odds are you aren't properly keeping track of your weight. Assuming you are taking off and landing in a basically upright position, there are at least three ways you can get into trouble.

The most common is **upper body - lower body split.** If during takeoff or final approach you allow your lower body to fall to the right, the glider will turn in that direction. If you attempt to correct the turn by moving your upper body to the left, the glider will continue to turn right even if you've maintained proper airspeed. See Figure 14, following, for an illustration of this problem.

Another common problem is **twisting.** If you attempt to correct the same right turn discussed above by twisting your body on its vertical axis, the glider will continue to go right. The glider doesn't care that you are now facing left — your weight is still on the right. Twisting is illustrated by the pilot on the right of Figure 14, following.

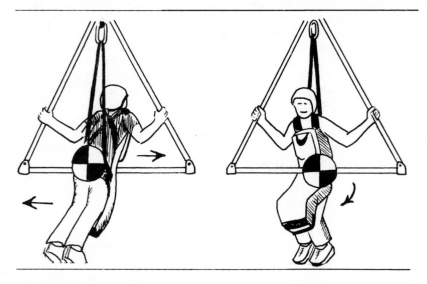

Figure 14. Upper-lower body split and twisting.

Passivity is another problem. If in the same right turn on take-off or final, you just let your body fall where it may, it will continue to fall to the right and aggravate the turn.

So if you are relaxed and still experiencing problems with corrective turns at takeoff or on final approach, think of your legs and hips, keeping your hips square to and equidistant from the basetube. Put your legs in the direction you want to go and the glider will follow.

PROBLEMS RELATED TO
CONCENTRATION AND FOCUSING

So you think you've conquered all the problems we've discussed so far but all of a sudden some of them start reappearing on an occasional and apparently random basis. Odds are you're experiencing concentration problems. As a relatively inexperienced pilot you are still having to concentrate on relaxing, controlling airspeed, and keeping track of your weight during the critical stages of launch and landing. It's not automatic yet. As you start to shift some of your concentration to trying new maneuvers, soaring, or whatever, you may regress in terms of your launch and landing proficiency simply because you're distracted by the new stuff you're trying to accomplish.

If this happens to you, you simply have to re-focus on basic launch and landing skills. A good perspective to maintain in this regard is to realize that the number one way to get hurt or killed in a hang glider is through hard contact with the ground and the two primary ways to accomplish that are to screw up a takeoff or a landing.

PROBLEMS RELATED TO
JUDGMENT OF CONDITIONS

Well, we're back to the same old bottom line. Taking off or getting into a position where you have to land in conditions you are not sure you can handle virtually guarantees problems. If you have solid Novice level skills, that's great for Novice level conditions. If you ask yourself to execute Advanced level skills through the decision to launch in Advanced level conditions, you are begging for trouble because you're leaving yourself absolutely no margin for error. Consult the USHGA Pilot Proficiency Rating System, discussed in Article 3, for specifics on skill levels vis-a-vis operating limitations.

Use good judgment in deciding where and when to launch (considering what you're likely to have to land in) and you'll live to be an old hang glider pilot. Use bad judgment and at best you'll have some outrageous war stories. At worst you'll get your name in the annual review of careless pilots who purchased the farm.

8. Going Prone

Growing Pone — er, uh — Going Prone is the topic for this article. Yes indeed, we are going to discuss at length that seemingly innocent to and fro transition between your basic "Neanderthal slouch" that we all take off and land in and the ultra cool "Superman en route to Lois Lane" prone position that most of us like to fly around in.

The prone transition, much maligned and maladroitly misused by many, is a subject that bears some looking into not only from a technique viewpoint but from a larger, perhaps more philosophical, perspective.

For instance, your average street thinker might observe: "I mean, like fer sure man, everyone like knows it's a total heart attack to watch some stirrup/cocoon banzai cowboy punch into a hill in the downwind stall mode while thrashing around in search of some tubular foot rest he barely avoided tripping over in, like, the first freaking place."

And so the question posed by members of The Church of the Wholly Redeeming Knee Hanger might be, to wit: "And lo, it seems to us that if we are capable of designing and using harnesses that make the transition from running upright to flying prone an automatic affair then are we not like unto imbeciles if we do not use these harnesses exclusively?"

To which our ever-lovin' Sturrup Cowboy, a major "flosifer", responds: "Well sonny, yuh jes' maht have the makins of a point thar if'n it warn't fer the fact that them thar knee whangers of your'n kinda hog tie yer lags t' yer shoulder chucks an' kinda, sorta puts a hitch t' yer get along, if'n yuh take mah meanin'."

Never one to miss an intense philosophical debate, the mystic BaBa Spa Gheti Dangleer chimes in: "YesYes but I have seen the many children of Co Coon meditate too long on the positional fluctuations of their footshrines."

"Yeah, but you knee banger doods look funny when you try to take off in dead air on a shallow slope or land a hi-performance glider in anything but a hurricane headwind," yells "Spud" the USHGA observer. And on, and on, and on.

Wanna know how it really is? Wanna hear the gospel according to my very own personal stinking opinion? You have no choice! Stop whining!

Knee hanger, Spaghetti type harnesses that connect your shoulders or upper body to your legs below the knees via a pulley or ring system are inherently inferior to stirrup and conventional cocoon harnesses. The reason they are inferior is that they inhibit the freedom of motion of your legs and make it more difficult for you to run all the way through a takeoff (especially dead air, shallow slope), execute a complete flare, or run out a mistimed landing. If your legs are tied to your upper body all you have to do is lean forward on takeoff and your legs are yanked out from under you. On landing you have to force your legs down (against the weight of your upper body) by applying downward pressure on the control bar. It has taken the advent of fast, double surface fixed airfoil gliders to expose the glaring weaknesses of such harness systems in light-to-no-wind situations.

The only real advantage to knee hanger type harnesses seems to be that they avoid the hair raising issues posed by the infamous prone transition phase of flying with a stirrup/cocoon harness system. That brings us back to the purpose of this article, which is to outline a system which takes the YIKES! out of the prone transition and thereby destroys the only quasi-legitimate argument in favor of knee hanger harnesses.

All of this represents my own opinion which, of course, is very true.

THE RAP AGAINST STIRRUP/COCOON HARNESSES

I can almost hear my momma tellin' me after watchin' me pull off some routine kid-o-batic manuever: "Son, I know a boy who got his eye put out that way." I grew up believin' that half the world's population knew my momma and had at least one glass eye. Now that I'm mostly grown up I get the same feelin' listenin' to knee banger guys say: a) I saw a guy stall his launch whilst lookin' for his stirrup, b) I saw a guy turn into the hill whilst lookin' for his cocoon boot, c) I saw a guy run into another guy whilst lookin' for his feet, or d) I saw a guy who couldn't even find his stirrup for a whole flight. Haw Haw. Whatta Geek! Wonder if he lived?

Sigh--------All too true. Too many people fall prey to the classic stirrup trap which is to figure that it's so important to get prone quick that it's OK to ignore airspeed, terrain, traffic, attitude of the glider and other life and death variables for a short time until one is "safely" (read coolly, quickly, or cleanly) proned out.

The main problem is that people tend to become focused on locating, immobilizing, and pushing into a stirrup or boot and lose their concentration on maintaining straight, level flight at an airspeed appropriate to conditions. Another way to put it is as follows: Hang glider pilots have been known to inadvertently alter their glider's airspeed or attitude in the process of doing transitions between prone and basic takeoff positions. Of course any time one "inadvertently" alters one's airspeed or attitude just after takeoff or just before landing, one is essentially not unlike a person soaked in gasoline who is in the process of discovering matches.

There are two solutions to this problem. The first is to weld this thought to your heart and mind: Next to forgetting to hook in on a cliff launch, losing control of your glider while trying to go prone is the most foolish and unnecessary thing you can do in a hang glider. There are virtually no penalties whatsoever for remaining in the basic takeoff, landing position until you're damn good and ready to go prone smoothly, confidently, and WITHOUT losing concentration on airspeed and attitude. You can ridge soar, thermal, and drive around all day in the basic takeoff, landing position. There is no good reason to be in a frinking (freaking, stinking) hurry to get prone — so don't be.

The second solution is to find and use a technique that allows you to locate, immobilize, and push into your stirrup/boot without ever losing track of or inadvertently changing your glider's airspeed and attitude. Whatever technique you select, practice it on the ground at least dozens of times before you try it in the air.

What follows, for your consideration, is a discussion of the technique we use to teach prone transitions to our students. It is a technique that we've been using for years. I learned it from Don (Double Daddy) Burns who used to work for me before he decided he should get a job that would allow him to feed BOTH of his babies on a regular basis.

DA SYSTEM

Quite simple to outline actually. It breaks the prone transition into three stages and asks the pilot to do a quick check to assure that the glider is straight, level, and at a proper airspeed (trim in most instances) before proceeding to the next step.

And so:

1. Pilot launches and remains in the basic takeoff-landing position while checking the glider for straight, level, and trim.

2. Pilot, still looking straight ahead, locates and immobilizes stirrup or boot, then checks again for straight, level, and trim.

3. Pilot pushes into harness, simultaneously transitions hands (one at a time or both together depending on conditions), and again checks for straight, level and trim.

We have found that by forcing our students to think about three checks for straight, level, and trim and by emphasizing the check part of the prone transition (as opposed to the locate, immobilize, and push parts) we can minimize their natural tendencies to go for the stirrup immediately, look back, push up, pull in, or push out during their first transitions. It's perfectly OK for the transition to take a fair amount of time, or not even occur at all because mechanical problems can always be addressed in practice. Naturally, we have the pilots practice the mechanics of location, immobilization, and pushing in on a simulator prior to having them try it in the air, and naturally we insist that they simulate their three critical checks as well.

DA ELEMENTS

Straight and Level. Gets the pilot safely away from the hill as the transition is in progress. Many pilots violate this rule in an effort to stay near a ridge. They end up hurrying into prone or transitioning while turning to stay in the lift band. A better option is to stay in the basic takeoff position, do your initial few passes to get safely ABOVE (as opposed to out from) terrain, and then go prone. You do not have to be prone to climb in even marginal ridge lift.

Trim. A series of checks for trim speed accomplishes the following: It forces the pilot to relax and minimizes his tendency to support weight on the downtubes while going prone. It is, of course, undesireable to support weight on the downtubes because you will be likely to pull your glider into a turn when it comes time to transition your hands to the basetube. Focusing on trim also encourages a pilot to maintain a smooth, consistent, appropriate airspeed during the transition. Flying way too fast can cause over-control problems and flying way too slow is obviously unspeakably dangerous. Flailing back and forth on the control bar during prone transition nicely combines the worst of both options.

The trim reference, of course, is not absolute. Sometimes you'll have to carry a little more speed and sometimes you can get away with a little less. For MOST conditions, however, you should be right around trim as you go into or out of prone.

Location/Immobilization of Stirrup or Cocoon. The trick is to find and make stationary the stirrup bar or cocoon boot. Your goal is to get into a position where you are ready to push into the harness. There is only one way to do so with a cocoon harness and that is to stick your knee to the side as illustrated in Figure 15, and hook the boot with your foot. There are a variety of ways to get a foot on a stirrup bar and most involve your knee or shin. Much depends on your build, flexibility, and harness adjustment. If your harness is adjusted to your taste and you find it impossible to get a foot on your bar or in your boot, don't despair. Just tie a loop to the bottom and use it like you would a ladder.

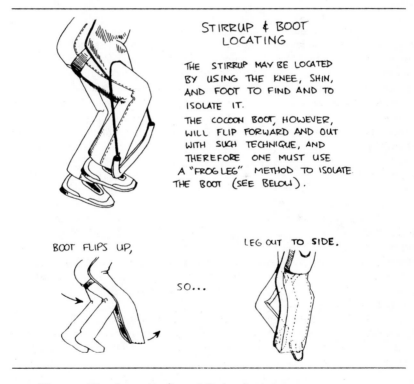

STIRRUP & BOOT
LOCATING

THE STIRRUP MAY BE LOCATED BY USING THE KNEE, SHIN, AND FOOT TO FIND AND TO ISOLATE IT.

THE COCOON BOOT, HOWEVER, WILL FLIP FORWARD AND OUT WITH SUCH TECHNIQUE, AND THEREFORE ONE MUST USE A "FROG LEG" METHOD TO ISOLATE THE BOOT (SEE BELOW).

BOOT FLIPS UP,

SO...

LEG OUT TO SIDE.

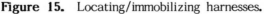

Figure 15. Locating/immobilizing harnesses.

Pushing Into the Harness. This is easy and fun. All you have to do is develop the ability to do it without doing a violent push up (or out, or down, or in) on the control bar. You may need a little control bar leverage to push into the harness but you shouldn't need much. If you cannot push into prone without wrestling with the control bar, look into getting a different harness. Practice in a simulator or in your garage using a chair for a control bar.

Dropping Out of Prone. The same principles apply. Do it with sufficient (at least 50') ground clearance, do it without wrestling your control bar, and keep track of your airspeed and attitude. Don't worry about tripping on your boot or stirrup during landing. So long as the glider is flying and supplying tension to your harness mains, the boot or stirrup is well up and out of the way of your feet.

MORE ON TRIPPIN'

You need to have a method for keeping your boot or stirrup out of the way of your feet on launch. This is especially true for light wind or no wind launches in which you need to take two or more steps before the glider is supporting its own weight and supplying tension to the harness.

Figure 16 illustrates three possible methods. (Although the figure depicts a cocoon, the techniques apply equally well to stirrup harnesses.)

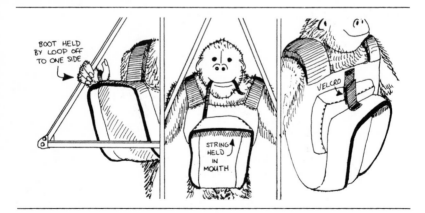

Figure 16. Keeping boot or stirrup out of the way.

Of the three methods illustrated the least desirable is the velcro method because it usually requires that the pilot grab and yank the velcro loose. One word of caution about the hold to the side method. If you take me at my word and decide not to go prone for an entire flight (just for the hell of it) be sure you let your boot or stirrup drop from your hand before you have to flare. One student of mine forgot to do so, attempted a flare, and wound up landing on a wing because his stirrup, still firmly in hand, inhibited his pushout on one side. Far out, no?

SUMMARY

The prone transition is not such a big deal that it should be avoided altogether through the use of knee hanger type harnesses which tie a pilot's legs (below the knees) to his shoulders, thereby limiting the mobility of his legs. This is especially true in reference to modern, faster, higher performing hang gliders that require an ability to run through a takeoff, run out a landing, and flare precisely and completely.

The prone transition for stirrup/cocoon harnesses does not have to be difficult or dangerous especially since there is no good reason to hurry and no compelling reason to accomplish the act of "getting prone."

Simply find and use a technique that forces you to pay primary attention to airspeed and attitude throughout your prone transitions and odds are you will never have to meet my momma or wear a glass eye. Byenow.

9. Exploring Your Glider's Speed Range

In this article we're going to tie up some loose ends which were generated by the last few articles on launch and landing techniques. More specifically, we're going to talk about airspeed recognition and control in a way that we hope will give the Novice pilot answers to the following burning questions:

1. What are minimum sink and best glide anyway?

2. Where do minimum sink and best glide live on my control bar?

3. Why doesn't Right Stuff mess with airspeed indicators, stall buzzers, etc. during his Novice days?

4. Why should I explore the entire speed range of my glider and how can I do so without pounding?

YOUR GLIDER'S SPEED RANGE

Let's start with a few definitions, keeping in mind that airspeed refers exclusively to the velocity of the flow of air over the surface of your wing. Figure 17, following, illustrates the flight paths resulting from various airspeeds.

Stall Speed. The minimum airspeed required to sustain flight. As you approach stall speed your glider will become somewhat less responsive. As you go below stall speed your glider will become significantly less responsive (maybe even totally out of control) and you will have a sensation of falling.

Minimum Sink Speed. The airspeed at which your rate of descent, usually expressed in feet per minute, is the lowest. Minimum sink speed on most gliders is only slightly above stall speed and is the speed at which experienced pilots like to execute soaring turns, especially in light lift conditions. Because of its proximity to stall speed (loss of control) it is not a good speed at which Novice pilots should be practicing turns. In most gliders, there is kind of a "floating along" sensation to minimum sink speed.

Best Glide Speed. The airspeed at which your glider will perform the best in terms of horizontal distance covered through the air per each unit of vertical descent. Best glide is slightly above minimum sink speed. If you fly at best glide speed and your clone flies at minimum sink speed on the same kind of glider in the same conditions, you fly the farthest but your clone will be in the air longest. The sensation of best glide in most gliders is that of cruising along in a crisply responding vehicle.

Fast Flight. Any speed from slightly above best glide to stuffing the bar to your knees. Your glider will feel increasingly more squirrely the faster you fly it and you will have the sensation of diving at the ground. Other clues of fast flight are increased pressure holding the control bar in and excessive noise.

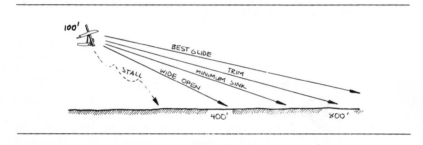

Figure 17. Flight paths at various airspeeds.

TRIM SPEED - YOUR PRIMARY REFERENT

There is one more very important speed to discuss and that is TRIM SPEED, or the speed at which your glider will fly if you simply let go of the bar and let it do its own thing. Different models of gliders trim at different speeds, either because of differences in design or in individual tuning. A vast majority of gliders are "trimmed" between minimum sink and best glide airspeeds.

Trim speed is your main point of reference in exploring your glider's speed range. It is essential that you know where you glider trims in order to determine where minimum sink and best glide live on your control bar.

The obvious corollary to the above statement is that it is extremely important that your glider is tuned properly (trims where it is supposed to). If you have any questions or doubts about your glider's intended trim speed and/or state of tune you should arrange for a professional dealer or the equivalent to fly and tune your glider.

TUNING INTO YOUR GLIDER'S SPEED RANGE

So now you know the main reference points in your glider's speed range and their position relative to one another. You also know where your make of glider trims in relation to the speed range and that your glider is properly tuned. You may now be wondering why Right Stuff didn't give you any numbers to attach to each of the speeds discussed and/or why Right Stuff doesn't recommend the use of airspeed indicators at the Novice level.

The answer to question one is: The particular airspeed values for stall, minimum sink, and best glide vary from model to model and from individual to individual. For instance, a heavier wing loading on a given glider makes all its speeds slightly higher than the same glider lightly loaded. Therefore, Right Stuff can't give you specific airspeed numbers that will be accurate for you.

There are two main reasons why Right Stuff does not recommend that you strap an airspeed indicator to your glider and go find your own numbers.

First, there is always a discrepancy between the airspeed indicated at the control bar (where you must mount the instrument in order to see it) and the actual airspeed over the wing. Simply put, an airspeed reading taken at the control bar is likely to be as much as 8 mph lower than the actual airspeed over the wing. Furthermore, the discrepancy is greater at the lower end of the speed range where an accurate reading is most critical. At higher speeds the discrepancy dwindles to 2-4 mph.

The second and most compelling argument against airspeed indicators for Novices is that the process of paying attention to the instrument creates more problems than it can possibly solve. If Wrong Stuff's eyes are riveted to his airspeed indicator he will not be hearing, feeling, and seeing what is going on around him. Sight, sound, and feel are by far the most reliable airspeed indicators available to the hang glider pilot.

In the original The Right Stuff, Tom Wolfe recounts an actual example of a jet test pilot diving his airplane into the ground while religiously reading and recording information from his instrument panel. Instruments, particularly airspeed indicators, don't tell you where the ground is.

SIGHT, SOUND, AND FEEL

So use your airspeed indicator to tell you how hard the wind is blowing at launch but leave it off your glider until you can AUTOMAT-ICALLY determine your airspeed by sight, sound, and feel.

Sight. Check out your control bar position in relation to your body. Note where the base tube is at trim speed. Note where it is when the glider starts to feel sluggish (stall), where it is during "controlled floating" (minimum sink), where it is at best glide, and where it is during fast flight. See Figure 18.

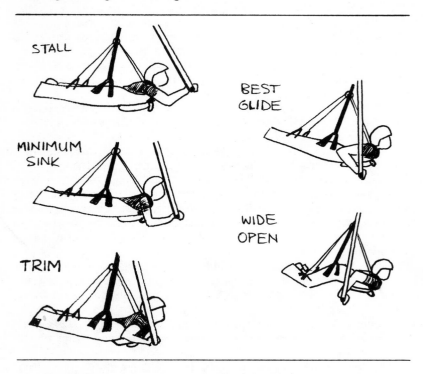

Figure 18. Control bar relative to body at various speeds.

Sound. Silence is death if you're close to the ground because silence means you're stalled and out of control. Note what your glider sounds like when it's sluggish, floating, cruising, and diving.

Feel. Note how much effort it takes to roll the glider at trim, and at all other speeds. The faster you fly the quicker the glider will respond to your weight shifting. Once again, see, hear and feel your speed range. Use trim as home base and put all the sights, sounds, and sensations together.

WHY YOU SHOULD EXPLORE YOUR SPEED RANGE

You should become totally familiar with how your glider behaves at all speeds so you won't ever be surprised if you have to act quickly to avoid pounding. If you've never felt how quick a fast moving glider turns you won't know that your best chance of avoiding a ridge is to speed up and then execute a snap turn (more on that later). If you've never felt a stall and a stall recovery you won't recognize it happening 50 feet off the ground where anything short of instant response is too late. If you don't know the difference between best glide and chocolate pudding you won't be able to get out of a canyon some day. And so on.

HOW YOU CAN EXPLORE YOUR SPEED RANGE WITHOUT POUNDING

Do it well away from any obstacles and do it in calm, non-lifting conditions. Start with trim speed and work slightly faster and slower from there. Do not work radically faster or slower unless you have at least 500-1000' of ground clearance and always be prepared to mellow back out at slightly faster than trim.

Above all:

> *Don't run out of altitude, airspeed, and ideas all at the same time.*

10. Intermediate Syndrome

In this article we're going to dredge up and re-examine the concept of Intermediate Syndrome. As recently as a few years ago Intermediate Syndrome was easily recognized and well understood. The evolution of hang glider technology and instructional technique, however, has created a situation which calls for a practical redefinition of the Intermediate Syndrome.

The underlying concept hasn't changed. Intermediate Syndrome was, is, and always will be the tendency of a relatively inexperienced hang glider pilot to become so overwhelmed by the exhilaration of flight that he forgets or ignores his own limitations and those of his equipment. What HAS changed are the nuts and bolts of Intermediate Syndrome: the way it shows up in today's pilots and gliders.

THE OLD INTERMEDIATE SYNDROME

Yesterday's Intermediate Syndrome, in retrospect, was brightly illuminated by yesterday's limitations in instructional technique and glider technology. Yesterday's beginner either bought a kit and survived his own trial and error training program or took two lessons from a professional and considered himself trained. To understate the point, there was a good deal of variation in the actual competence of newly "trained" pilots who appeared at demanding sites in demanding conditions. Those who screwed up were said to have fallen prey to Intermediate Syndrome.

Yesterday's gliders: Before 1979 new hot ones came out every 3-6 months. Some were certified, some were almost certified, and some were so slick that no one cared about certification. All were available to anyone who had the money. There was "Equipment Intermediate Syndrome," or, relatively inexperienced pilots inadvertently exploring the envelopes of inadvertently experimental equipment.

Intermediate Syndrome in the old days was highly visible because in addition to referring to poor judgment it tended to be a catch-all explanation for accidents that by today's standards could be more accurately attributed to: a) inadequate basic training, b) inadequate equipment or poor judgment in equipment selection, or c) inadequate information.

Another important point about yesterday's gliders, even post-1979 gliders which passed significantly tougher certification standards, has to do with their handling and performance characteristics. Simply put, the handling/performance coupling of older gliders made them fairly tough for the average Novice pilot to jump into and immediately soar. Time, patience, and skill were required to maximize their soaring potential and the net result was Novice pilots accumulating a fair amount of sled ride air time between their basic training and first soaring flights.

THE NEW INTERMEDIATE SYNDROME

The new Intermediate Syndrome is not as dramatically visible as the old one because it is not used nearly as much to account for accidents attributable to poor basic training and inferior equipment.

These days the average number of lessons taken by the average beginner has risen sharply. Assuming the area I operate in is somewhat representative of a national trend, I can safely say that the average student completes between 5 and 15 lessons before being turned loose on his own equipment. Consequently, there is noticeably less variation in the competence of newly trained pilots appearing on the hill and the average competence level is noticeably higher than it was a few years ago.

The equipment new pilots appear with is almost always certified to standards considerably higher than those of the '70's and is therefore inherently safer from a structural and aerodynamic point of view.

In regard to the relationship between glider design and Intermediate Syndrome, however, the most significant design changes have been in the areas of performance and handling characteristics. Today's ships do significantly better than older ships in terms of effective soaring potential which is basically a function of maneuverability and wing aerodynamic efficiency. More and more Novice pilots are jumping on state-of-the-art gliders, launching easily, soaring easily, and having only slight problems on landing. First soaring flights, even first cross country flights are taking place earlier and earlier in a pilot's career.

The result is an insidious, subtle brand of modern Intermediate Syndrome. Inexperienced pilots are very quickly exposed to the exhilaration of soaring flight. It is a heady experience to cross deep canyons, blithely hop ranges, gain thousands of feet in a thermal and stay up for hours. In the meantime soaring skills develop quickly while launch and landing skills atrophy from lack of practice. You no longer have to do multiple sled rides to satiate your flying appetite. The allure of soaring coupled with marginal launch and landing skills and limited experience in judging conditions makes for some pretty deadly combinations among modern pre-Intermediate pilots.

HOW TO BEAT THE NEW INTERMEDIATE SYNDROME

1. Continue to practice and refine launch and landing technique. Solicit and accept feedback from instructors, friends, and pilots more experienced than you.

2. If you've launched and landed 4 times in a given month and have 8 hours of airtime to show for it, go to the training hill and do 10 launches and landings.

3. Do not fly conditions you are not ABSOLUTELY sure of and comfortable with, specifically in terms of your launch and landing skills. FORGET the day's soaring potential when you make this decision.

4. Assume that most other pilots are more experienced than you. If they're flying a given set of conditions that doesn't necessarily mean you should. If you see them not flying in conditions you are considering flying — pack it up.

5. Be extra cautious and conservative the next time you fly after you've wowed yourself with a substantial altitude gain and a two-hour flight.

6. Remember that the very exhilaration you feel after a soaring flight (and maybe expect to feel next time) can cloud your judgment and make you a victim of Intermediate Syndrome. It only takes once.

11. The Legend of the Wuffo

Have you ever been fumbling around trying to set up your glider at the top of a hill you've never flown before (or in conditions you're just barely ready for) and overheard some jaded Hang IV veteran ask his equally smug buddy "Who is the 'wuffo' over there?" Chances are they're looking at you because you're not exhibiting sufficient non-chalance as you go through your set-up and pre-flight ritual. You've probably picked up on the fact that the use of the term "wuffo" in this particular context is meant to convey a certain amount of disrespect. Furthermore, the designation of you as a "wuffo" carries an unspoken designation of them as OK guys with credentials that qualify them to pass judgment on your competence as a hang glider pilot and worth as a human being.

Your response to this may range from wondering what "wuffo" means anyway to feeling unfairly put down, to a vigorous physical interpretation of how Johnny Cash's boy named Sue might deal with these two jerks. The fact remains you've been called a "wuffo" and you feel insulted. What you may not be aware of is that you've finally been exposed to a significant piece of hang gliding lore and culture. Woofdom is the subject of this article. Read on and you will be immeasureably enriched.

DERIVATION

The admittedly obscure derivation of the term "wuffo" is simply the contraction of two words and a question mark: what for? Some of the various spellings of this contraction are: whuffo, whufo, wofo, woofo, wooffo, and the very popular wuffo! Starting out life as a noun (he is a wuffo) it has recently been widely used as a verb (he wuffed that landing) and in the exclamatory form WOOF!

HISTORY

In the beginning, during the Genesis chapter of hang gliding history, there were two kinds of people. Group A did it and Group B asked Group A "What for do you do it?" Members of Group B never tired of bombarding members of Group A with increasingly astonishing variations of the basic "What for?" question. And lo, questions such as "Don't your arms get tired?" and "How do you guys breathe up there?" were born. In the privacy and comfort of their own company, members of Group A began to refer to members of Group B as "wuffos." Members of Group B, of course, already had a few choice names for members of Group A ranging from the polite "daredevils" to the more succinct "crazy bastards." And so it was for thousands, hundreds, maybe even three or four years.

And then, slowly, an assimilation began to occur. Remember (or maybe you don't remember) how American flag decals used to be the symbol of upstanding, America love it or leave it, moral conservatism? Remember how hippiedom and yippiedom neutralized and defactionalized this symbol by plastering flag decals on their VW vans and flag patches on their jeans? How about the nation's peace officers adopting the derisive pig symbol given them by hippiedom? Today's cops make pig jokes among themselves and I swear I actually met a cop who wore a pig tie tack.

So it was with hang glider pilots, but with an interesting twist. They didn't adopt a derogatory term bestowed upon them by someone else (pig). They didn't adopt someone else's positive symbol thereby neutralizing it (flag). Instead, hang glider pilots began to use on each other the same derogatory term they used on others. Hang glider pilots decided they were having so much fun calling wuffos wuffos that it stood to reason they could have even more fun calling each other wuffos.

To argue that such reasoning is ample evidence of the suicidal self destructive nature of hang glider pilots is to grossly underestimate the philosophical depth of Group A crazy bastards. Hang glider pilots simply discovered and embraced a profound truth of the human condition and enshrined this truth through their internalization of the term "wuffo."

WUFFO? POSITIVELY!

The truth is we are all wuffos! Furthermore it is good to be a wuffo because if you aren't you'll never learn anything.

The details are as follows.

1. Responsible hang glider pilots naturally strive to become better hang glider pilots.

2. Part of striving is screwing up.

3. The best thing to do when you screw up it to say "what for?"

4. This makes you a wuffo.

So there it is. You strive, screw up, be a wuffo, strive some more, screw up some more (at a higher level of competence of course), and be a wuffo. If you keep your screw ups relatively minor, and your what fors relevant to your screw ups, you can be a wuffo forever.

SUMMARY

The two guys who called you a wuffo at the beginning of this article were right! Right?

12. About Cool

This article is about cool. Emily Post would swear we're talking about etiquette here but then she never spent any time begging people to drive her up dusty rutted roads to obscure mountain tops so she could battle her way through 15 excited humans and their hang gliders to a small patch of ground where she could hook into her hang glider and run off into space. She also never spent any time mixing it up on a ridge or in a thermal with 15 other fanatics whose goal, like hers, was to get up as high and stay up as long as possible.

Sorry Emily, but when we're talking pursuit of airtime, words like "etiquette" or "manners" just don't get it. "Rules" is close but "cool" is what we're really talking about. So if you want to know what's cool and what's uncool in and around hang gliders, read on. You'll be immeasurably enriched.

DRIVERS AND RIDES UP THE HILL

Let's start at the beginning. If you're what those ultralight power boys disdainfully call a purist (no engines, man), you've got to get yourself and your glider up the hill. Unless you're lucky enough to fly a site where you can always land on top you've also got to be picked up where you land. Traditionally, getting to launch and getting picked up involve either a driver or the creative begging of rides.

All drivers should be treated with the utmost respect. A driver makes it possible for you to enjoy your whole hang gliding day. On the way out you don't have to worry about getting to the top. While flying you don't have to worry about landing out or landing in time to catch a ride to retrieve your vehicle. After landing you don't have to go through the time and effort of vehicle retrieval.

Driver privileges should include: the best seat in the car, exemption from contribution for gas, free burgers and beer, enthusiastic and sincere gratitude (just short of groveling), and other personal comforts such as lounge chairs, lemonade, and shark repellant.

It is definitely uncool to lead drivers to believe they're lucky to get a chance to come watch you spread your ego across the sky. It is also in poor form to take off leaving your driver with equipment strewn from one end of launch to the other, without directions to the landing area (or enough gas to get there), and with the comment: "Everything works fine except for the brakes." If you don't tie extra gliders onto the rack or if you forget to leave keys, you get what you deserve.

If you're not lucky enough to have a driver it's usually easy to cadge rides from your pilot brothers and sisters who, like you, know what's at stake. Your chances of getting rides are increased if you don't EXPECT people to wait for you, overload their car or rack, or do it for nothing, though lots of times they'll do all three. More specifically, it is incumbent upon you to load up quickly and offer gas money or other compensation for the favor. It's sort of uncool to ask for a car retrieval ride to the top after dark. If you have to do so occasionally you will probably get your ride because most pilots are more than willing to help out in a pinch.

SET UP AREA AND LAUNCH

Set up so that you won't directly interfere with someone who staked out a set-up area before you. It's basically first come, first served. If you like to set up early and wait for conditions to get better do both at a place where others can get by you to launch.

If you're hooked in and standing at launch waiting for the right moment to start your takeoff run, by all means take your time. If you're taking a longer time than is normal for you it is definitely cool to tell the person behind you that you're not comfortable with current conditions and ask if he'd like to launch ahead of you. If you're waiting behind someone whom you feel is taking an inordinate amount of time to launch, it is cool to tell the person that you like current conditions and ask if you can take off ahead of him. It is totally uncool to pressure him, question his manhood, or make derisive comments about him and his momma (or to pressure her, question her womanhood, or make derisive comments about her poppa, if he's a she).

RIDGE LIFT

Time to get serious. The difference between being cool and being uncool while working ridge lift can literally be the difference between life and death. The basic rules are as follows:

1. When two gliders approach each other head on at the same level, always give way to the right (turn to the right). If one goes right and the other left, a mid-air collision is likely.

2. Unless you are ABSOLUTELY sure no one else is near you, make your passing turns AWAY from the ridge (into the wind!). Turning into the ridge puts you on a downwind leg which means

you'll cover more airspace before coming out of the turn. Space is limited on a ridge. Also, while you're barging through all that space, your bank angle keeps you blind to traffic until a split second before you come out of the turn. In Figure 19, the glider turning away from the ridge is blind to traffic over less space and through less of his turn arc than is the glider turning into the ridge.

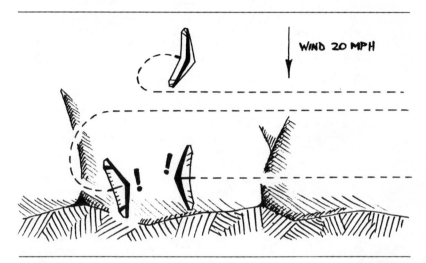

Figure 19. Passing turns in ridge lift.

3. When two gliders are traveling in the same direction, at the same level, the overtaking (faster) glider passes on the ridge side. This works well with rule two because when the glider in front follows rule two and makes his passing turn away from the ridge, the overtaking glider does not interfere with the turn. In Figure 20, following, a glider being overtaken has just completed a proper passing turn away from the ridge. The glider attempting to overtake him toward the ridge is safe, but the glider overtaking to the outside is on a collision course.

Figure 20. Passing another glider in ridge lift.

4. A glider coming up has the right of way. The higher glider must give way because he's the only one who can see what's going on. The glider coming up in Figure 21; the top one can.

Figure 21. Giving way to glider coming up.

5. In any event clear all turns and constantly look around. DO NOT stare straight down or at your vario. Fly as though anyone at any time could violate these rules. Always leave yourself room to get away from traffic.

6. Specific ridges may have specific rules. Torrey Pines, for example, requires that all pilots carry whistles which must be blown to signal takeoff, passage through the RC glider window, and intent to approach for landing. Check with locals for specifics.

THERMAL LIFT

Same life and death situation. The basic rules are as follows:

1. The first person entering the thermal establishes the direction of the turn. Figure 22 shows the obvious problem of two pilots turning in opposite directions. Right: Gliders can see each other most of the time and, by traveling in the same direction, are not on a collision course. Wrong: Gliders are blind to each other due to their bank angles and are on a collision course.

Figure 22. Circling in same direction in shared thermal.

2. Enter the thermal at different levels. For example, it is cool to allow the glider preceding you a few turns to gain altitude before entering yourself.

3. Do not cut the circle of other gliders in the same thermal. Adjust to other gliders so that your circles are more or less concentric. Figure 23, following, illustrates this rule. Right: None of the gliders is cutting the others' circles. Wrong: All gliders are turning in the same direction but their circles all intersect and there's a high risk of collision at the intersection.

4. The glider on top must give way to a glider coming up from below for the same reason illustrated in Figure 21.

5. Always clear turns and constantly look around. Do not stare straight down or at your vario. Assume people will violate these rules and always leave yourself room to escape from traffic.

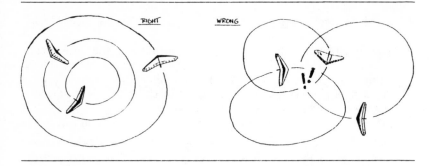

Figure 23. Adjusting to other gliders in shared thermal.

6. Specific sites may have specific rules or characteristic conditions. Check with locals or more experienced pilots before flying new sites or attempting more demanding thermaling techniques.

SUMMARY

1. Treat drivers like gold. They're worth their weight in it.

2. Don't expect favors when begging rides from other pilots even though you usually can.

3. Be considerate of others during set up and launch.

4. Follow rules of the ridge and be cool in thermals. Don't count on anyone else to do likewise unless you know them and their degree of cool extremely well.

5. Clear all turns and constantly look around.

6. Know specific rules and characteristic conditions of specific sites BEFORE you fly.

7. Don't be in a big hurry — you have an entire soaring career in front of you.

13. Wind?!

Good old Bob Dylan once blurted: "Yuh doan need a weatherman to know which way the wind blows." McCartney and Lennon used to wail: "I'll get by with a little help from my friends."

Your average citizen, of course, has absolutely no reason to perceive the connection between these seemingly random refrains. Your average hang glider pilot, on the other hand, has not only a primal awareness of the basic truths contained in each lyric, but also a range of experience that confirms their interrelatedness.

Frinstance. How many Intermediate or better pilots do you know who have never had occasion to approach an unfamiliar LZ (or a familiar LZ in unfamiliar conditions) that has few or none of the traditional features used by hang glider pilots to determine wind velocity and direction? How many Intermediate or better pilots do you know who have never had to actually select a final approach turn direction based solely on information obtained from other pilots on the ground? In such situations, "Weathermen," of the kind Dylan contemptuously refers to, are clearly useless and a pilot's only hope becomes "a little help from his friends."

Now granted, such situations are not the norm. There's usually at least one windsock or some grass, trees, dust, smoke, or water to give us the necessary info about the wind. But sometimes — just sometimes — pilots in the air must rely on pilots on the ground to provide a quick, reliable signal indicating wind direction.

There has been much discussion as to just how pilots on the ground should go about the business of signaling to their brothers and sisters in the air. Letters to Hang Gliding magazine and discussions among various groups of pilots have outlined a welter of options involving some combination of facing into or away from the wind and gesturing (in some fashion or another) with or against its flow. Throw in the various ways to read gliders parked tail down or up, set into, with, or across the flow of the wind and you can see the possibilities for confused, not to mention tragically flawed, communication. See Figure 24, following.

Figure 24. Previous system for signaling wind direction.

Noting such possibilities the USHGA Safety and Training committee convened in Kansas City with the goal of creating a standard, USHGA approved, wind direction signal. Through a process that can only be described as "responsibly concerned hysterical consideration of all possible weird body positions and gestural sequences" your directors achieved their goal.

Ridiculously simple and impossible to misinterpret, the official USHGA "bend over and smile" wind direction indication technique involves the following: Face the wind, bend over 45 to 90 degrees at the waist, and extend the arms out and back like wings. In other words, just pretend that you, dear groundling, are an approaching hang glider. See Figure 25, following.

Figure 25. USHGA approved wind direction signal.

Your sky brother or sister, who really is an approaching hang glider, can immediately relate and quickly respond to your signal.

The more imaginative among us can even embellish the basic signal in creative ways. For instance, if wind in the LZ is switchy you can weathervane around the arc of the switchiness and make pecking motions with your head. (Do the funky chicken?) If gusty conditions prevail you can, in synch with the gusts, "Lean forward — bop, bop — lean back," a la Fats Domino. If thermals are breaking loose and the approach is likely to be bumpy you can do like old time rock n' roller Jerry Lee Lewis and "Shake it around jis' a little bit." And, hey, if conditions in the LZ are clearly unlandable (hurricanes, raging bulls, insurance salesmen) simply grab with both hands onto the place where your legs meet and fall to the ground writhing like a punk rocker. Once on the ground, if you think it proper, make repeated chute throwing motions with one hand while you continue to thrash about.

Finally, if you ever see Ned (High Tech in Texas) Negap on final approach anywhere, any time — whether he whines for wind direction or not — just assume he needs help and then assume the position.

And don't forget, dear reader, to pull down your pants just before you bend over. Ned likes it that way, he's used to it, and it's the only thing that'll make him land right side up, on his feet and ready to (how did the Crystals say it?) "de do run run."

P.S. I suppose If we're going to have a standard procedure for indicating wind direction we should also have a standard procedure for requesting an indication. While a casually drawled "Whut the hellzit doin down there?" is a fine expression of ennui, the piercing, plaintive exclamation "WIND?!" will probably get quicker results.

14. First Altitude Flights

Everybody remembers his or her first high altitude flight. For sheer intensity, the sensations and feelings associated with the antici- pation, consummation, and reminiscence of one's first altitude flight have got to rank right up there with those associated with the loss of one's virginity. It's the kind of thing that, by definition, happens only once, and unless you're really weird you'll never be the same again.

To quickly shift to the infinitely safer military analogy the ex- perience of first altitude flight is probably a lot like getting orders saying: "Ahem, the infantry no longer requires your services to jerk awkward 60-pound triangular dacron, pole objects off wretched little hills in hot weather. You are commanded to report immediately to Never Never Land where you will be required to stand momentarily on a serene mountain at the very top of the universe, bathe briefly in the cool, gentle breeze that will be there, and then emerge smoothly into an intimate, totally fulfilling (not to mention draining) relationship with the sky itself. Plus you don't have to carry the triangle, pole thing back up the mountain, soldier. Lt. Venus or Sgt. Adonis here will drive for you."

This article examines first altitude flights (FAFs): What consti- tutes an FAF? How does one prepare for it? What new issues do you face when you finally get to (how shall I say it?) "Get a little?"

WHAT IT IS

My first FAF happened when I finally stopped pounding the nose of my glider into the training hill and rocketed 5' into the air (stopped saying ick at the sight of girls). My second FAF was when I overshot the lip of the upper training hill where I was supposed to land and found myself suspended 30' in midair headed down the lower training hill (kissed Melinda Whatshername and ran for cover). My third FAF occurred when I ran off a hill called the 500' which was really a 350' and maintained 75' ground clearance most of the way to the LZ (making out: first base through third base).

My fourth FAF, which was really my first, no kidding, altitude flight was off a small mountain called the 1,500'. I knew I'd taken a big step then because everything was a LOT different than it had been before. (I wonder whatever happened to Ruthann?) I didn't know it at the time but the biggest difference was that in one flight I had increased my previous maximum ground clearance by more than 10 fold (from 75' to over 750'). It was a whole new ball game because it was a whole new perspective and it seemed to take forever. All my previous FAFs were really big deals at the time but they all took place in pretty much the same environment — within 75' of the ground.

The point of all this blather about my personal learning experience is to provide some rationale for the following definition of first altitude flight: The flight during which you can expect to achieve a maximum ground clearance that exceeds your previous maximum by a factor larger than any you'll ever experience. Usually it is also your longest flight by a wide margin.

If you live in a place with a 50' training hill and a 500' hill suitable for Novice pilots with nothing between or beyond, your first flight from the 500' will be your FAF. If you live in a place with hills suitable for Novices ranging from 75' to 300' to 500' to 3,000', the 3,000' will be your FAF. The point is, wherever you train to fly you must identify the site which will be "the big one" and plan accordingly.

HOW TO PREPARE FOR IT

Talk to girls if you're a boy, boys if you're a girl. Pass notes in class, flirt, kiss, grow hair in the right places. Get a deep voice or grow bumps in the right places depending on your gender. Give and receive hickies. Preparation is everything.

Hey! Get back here! The best way to prepare for your FAF is to have all Beginner and Novice level skills totally mastered before you even think of leaving the training hill. Smooth, clean launches in moderate to light to slightly crossed wind conditions should be nearly automatic. Landings should be consistently on your feet, wings level, into the wind, and within 100' of where you want to be. You should be able to judge general conditions and have a good working knowledge of micrometeorology. Recognition and smooth manipulation of airspeeds between minimum sink and slightly faster than best glide is mandatory. Mastery of immediate, appropriate corrective turns, purposeful S-turns, and linked 90-degree turns is a must. Also, you need to be well on your way to mastering 180-degree turns so that you can execute a reasonable landing approach the first time you fly high.

Perhaps most important of all you should be confident enough in your ability to perform the above tasks that you are basically relaxed in the air. If you aren't sure you're likely to have an attack of excessively high anxiety on your FAF.

Another important point is that you should know in advance where your FAF is going to take place in case there are specific additional skills you must have to fly the site safely. For example, Eastern pilots generally have to develop very precise landing approaches at the training hill because LZs in the East are generally smaller and more obstructed than those in the West.

Again, preparation is everything. The reason this is so is that when you embark on "Mission FAF" you need to be able to focus a good portion of your attention on dealing with anxiety, airspeed, and approaches in ways you've never had to in your previous hang gliding experience. You only have so much attention to go around. If you're focusing attention on launch deficiencies you won't have much left to give to the three A's of FAFing.

THE THREE A'S OF FAF-ING

Anxiety (Angst, highty). Anyone who tells you he was totally cool when it happened to him for the first time is LYING. No matter how well prepared you are there is a certain amount of anxiety involved in FAFing. I mean you may know you have the equipment and the skills to use it, but until you've actually done it you're not really sure you can. As I've noted before, anxiety can be either constructive or debilitating. Figure 26 illustrates the difference.

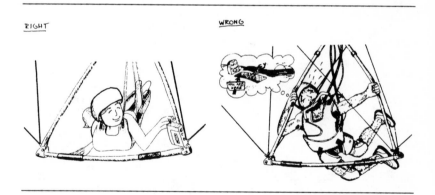

RIGHT   WRONG

Figure 26. Role of anxiety in first altitude flights.

If you haven't prepared well enough for your FAF and know it odds are you will be either unable to focus on the new tasks at hand or you will be generally tense and therefore unable to execute smoothly. If you haven't prepared and don't know it odds are you'll quickly discover your weaknesses on launch, in midair, or on approach. High anxiety, tension, poor execution, injury, or death is a typical sequence in the worst cases. If you have prepared well enough and know it you can use your pre-FAF anxiety to help you focus constructively on the new tasks at hand.

Airspeed. Usually FAFers tend to do it too fast and it's not because of eagerness either. FAFers are tempted to fly too fast because they are not used to an environment which features gobs of ground clearance and, relatively speaking, gobs of time in the air. It's obvious why more time in a strange environment makes one anxious: More time spent cheating death! More time to panic! Figure 27 shows why gobs of ground clearance tempt FAFers to fly faster than necessary.

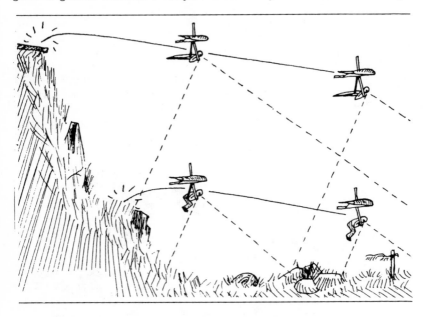

Figure 27. Ground clearance and the FAFer.

Briefly, it's because most Beginners, no matter how well they've been taught to judge airspeed by trim reference, sight, sound, feel, or airspeed indicators, tend to judge airspeed by ground reference. The higher you are at a given airspeed, the slower the ground SEEMS to be going by. You give somebody 750' ground clearance when they're used to 75', and ask them to fly at trim speed they'll feel like they're standing still. I know I did. It makes you WANT to pull in to get that ground going by faster. The trick is not to succumb to that temptation. Focus on good old trim reference, sight, sound, and feel to get your AS where you want it (between slightly faster than minimum sink and best glide).

I'll never forget one student of mine who was on the verge of but not quite ready for his FAF and I let him go anyway. He churns off the hill just fine, hauls the bar all the way in, and smokes on into the LZ over-controlling like there was no tomorrow. (Flying extremely fast makes it very difficult to avoid over-controlling.) So, I spend three lifetimes watching this guy make it safely to the LZ and drive down. He's standing next to his glider with a metal batten in his hand and he knows exactly what he did. He offers me the batten, saying "You wanna beat me now or later?" I, of course, deserved the beating for letting him FAF when he was less than totally prepared.

Approaches. Unprepared FAFers also tend to blow landing approaches. Sometimes even totally prepared FAFers blow approaches. Why? Because now it takes more than three or four turns to burn off enough altitude to put down close to where you want to be. Figure 28 shows a typical figure 8 or linked 180s landing approach.

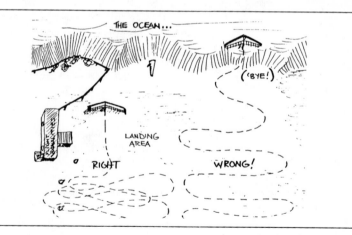

Figure 28. Figure 8 or linked 180s approach.

Proper execution of this approach involves burning off all but final approach turn altitude at the downwind end of the LZ. Touchdown then occurs in the middle of the LZ. Typical improper execution of the approach involves allowing the linked 180s to get progressively narrower. The pilot in this instance has put himself at the far end of the LZ with no room to land. Avoid this problem by doing a thorough job of scouting the LZ and picking out turn reference points in the terrain. Obviously the more mastery you have of 180-degree turns the better off you'll be.

SUMMARY

1. You will never forget your first altitude flight. If anyone asks you what it was like tell them it was like having sex for the first time only you were better prepared for the experience.

2. The best way to make your FAF a successful one is to be totally prepared for it. Have all Novice level skills mastered and be well on your way to mastering appropriate Intermediate level skills such as linked 180-degree turns. This will allow you to harness and use high anxiety in a constructive way.

3. Avoid the temptation to fly faster than needed by focusing on true airspeed indicators such as trim reference, sight, sound, feel, and (if you must) instruments. So what if it seems like you're stuck in a vat of molasses. It just means you get to stay up longer.

4. Avoid sloppy (trapped in a corner) landing approaches by scouting the LZ, picking out turn reference points, and working as much as possible on perfecting 180-degree turns.

5. Be absolutely sure to pick a proper site and proper conditions for your FAF. A proper site is one with a clear easy launch and an LZ that is easy to get to and put down in. Proper conditions are a light to moderate steady uphill breeze with minimal lift.

Thanks to Ken de Russy, Greg DeWolf, and Joe Greblo for their input to this article.

15. Pre-Soaring Skills

OK kids, no joking around. In this article we're gonna get right down to it. Listen. Once you put the training hill behind you and successfully complete your first few altitude flights you effectively enter the single most dangerous stage of your hang gliding career. No matter how well you've been trained, no matter how careful you perceive yourself to be, the fact is you are now more vulnerable to INADVERTENTLY getting in over your head than you ever have been or ever will be as long as you fly hang gliders.

Think about it. While training you are under direct professional supervision. You basically rely on your instructor to keep you from doing anything absolutely foolish. On the other end of the spectrum, once you've accumulated a fair amount of experience in a variety of conditions over a fair period of time, you develop a pretty good idea of what's going on. You may get in over your head but it probably won't be because you don't know any better. More experienced pilots generally get in trouble because they ignore the lessons of their experience or the limits of their skills.

No doubt about it. Between the training hill stage and the experienced Intermediate stage you are a lot like that lovable old cartoon character of legendary blindness, Mr. Magoo. For those of you under thirty who don't know Mr. Magoo from Adam, think of yourselves as a young Luke Skywalker. You're eager and ready to take on the whole universe of hang gliding and you think Darth Vadar is an overrated wimp. Worse, most parts of the Force aren't with you yet and you haven't even figured out if Yoda is simply an ugly dwarf or the seer he claims to be.

Well I've got news for you. Yoda IS the seer he claims to be. Furthermore, I've spoken directly with the boy and he's given me a list of skills and capabilities Novice pilots need to develop between the time they leave the training hill and the time they begin to work lifting air.

THE FIRST THING

In my opinion a pilot needs to accumulate 5-10 hours of airtime in conditions no stronger than the strongest he's experienced at his training hill before he should actively attempt to fly stronger (soarable) conditions. Such an approach gives a pilot an intact frame of reference for judging conditions. Simply, don't fly in conditions that your instructor would deem unsuitable for training were he with you.

Generally this means accumulating airtime in "sled ride" conditions (mild, non-lifting air) or in "extended sled ride" conditions (relatively smooth end-of-the-day lift). These are the ONLY conditions which are suitable for practicing the new skills you need to master BEFORE you attempt to work moderate to severe ridge or thermal lift.

AND ANOTHER THING

I'm not kidding. Do not practice any of these maneuvers in anything by mild, relatively smooth conditions. Have plenty of ground clearance (500' or more) and be comfortable enough with high altitude flying to be relaxed and confident in the air. If at all possible fly out to a point where the landing area is thoroughly visible and accessible before you begin practicing these maneuvers. This will minimize your chances of becoming disoriented and losing track of the LZ.

AIRSPEED

Now that you're going to be in the air 5-20 minutes at a time you'll want to spend part of it exploring your glider's speed range. Remember, trim speed is home base.

Low Speed. It is extremely important to thoroughly familiarize yourself with low speed flight because once you start working lift, you're going to be cheating slow so you can get higher and stay up longer than your buddies. The slower you fly, however, the more sluggish your glider's response to your attempts to turn it. There is a point at which you no longer have roll authority. Here's how you find it:

1. Start with straight, level, trim speed (SLT) flight. Note how your glider responds to your roll input.

2. Return to SLT. Push out slightly from trim and again note roll response when you shift your weight slightly from side to side.

3. Keep pushing out in small increments and noting roll response. (More pressure and more lag the slower you go.)

4. Note that at a certain point the glider will begin to mush and shortly thereafter you will find it almost impossible to roll the glider.

5. Allow the glider to return to trim speed and repeat the process until you can instantly recognize the point at which you lose roll authority.

6. Once you are comfortable pushing the glider right to the edge of stall, get good and relaxed and actually stall it. Start from trim and push slowly out until your arms are extended. The glider will mush, defining a progressively steeper glide path and then, somewhat suddenly, drop its nose to recover airspeed. When this happens, relax and allow the glider to return to trim position. **Do not repeat until you are back at SLT.** Figure 29 illustrates how the glider behaves when you stall it.

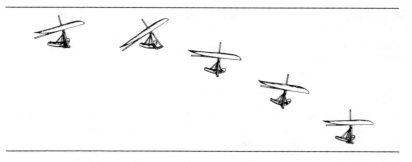

Figure 29. Stall progression.

Now you know how to recognize an impending stall, how to recover from it, and how the glider rolls at the low end of the speed range.

High Speed. It is also important to become thoroughly familiar with your glider's high speed flight characteristics. The glider will roll progressively quicker at progressively higher airspeeds, you will experience increasing pitch bar pressure, and you will learn that it is sometimes difficult to maintain a perfectly straight heading during the flight. You will also learn how much ground you can traverse and how much glide efficiency you can lose at higher airspeeds.

To explore the top end:

1. Start at SLT.

2. Gradually and progressively pull in noting roll rates and pressures at various speeds between trim and fast (control bar at navel). Also note increasing pitch pressure.

3. Try maintaining straight and level headings at progressively faster speeds.

4. Take note of increasingly fast progress over the ground vis-a-vis rate of vertical descent.

5. Smoothly, evenly, return to trim by gradually releasing pressure on the control bar.

Now that you have experienced the sensations and pressures associated with flying fast you won't be rattled by them when you have to make tracks someday to penetrate out of a canyon against a strong headwind.

TURNS

Another important area to explore during your 5-10 hours of sled ride airtime is turns. You say you learned how to turn smoothly at the training hill? True enough, but basically all your instructor was trying to do was coax you through low-banked coordinated turns resulting in 15- to 180-degree changes of heading. There wasn't enough altitude nor enough of your attention for him to teach you mushing turns, diving turns, and snap turns, all of which are useful for altitude manipulation and evasive maneuvering in addition to changes of heading.

See Figure 30, following, for glide paths achieved during different types of turns.

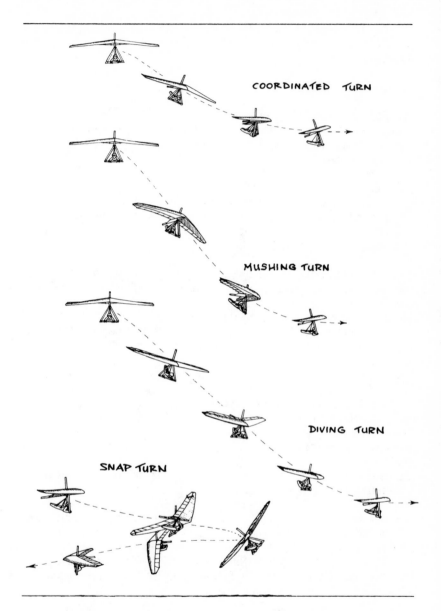

Figure 30. Coordinated, mushing, diving, and snap turns.

Coordinated Turns. By all means continue practicing these. I've found that most newer gliders coordinate fairly easily using the following method.

1. Start at SLT.

2. Pull in slightly (one or two inches will usually do) and simultaneously shift your weight to initate roll. The overall effect of this is to diagonally pull your weight toward a corner of the control bar.

3. Just after the glider starts to roll, return to the center of the bar and allow it to come out to a point where you feel no pitch pressure. Some gliders require light pushout to achieve coordination. You should be at this point be in a coordinated turn of about 15- to 20-degree bank angle.

4. Just before desired heading is achieved, pull your weight toward the opposite corner of the control bar to level the glider out.

5. Progressively steeper banked coordinated turns require that the roll input be held longer to achieve a steeper bank and they require more pushout to achieve coordination.

6. Do not exceed 30-degree bank angles at this stage of the game.

Mushing Turns. While trying to perfect coordinated turns you will undoubtedly perform some mushing turns. These are caused by too much pushout while in the turn. The sensation is literally a slipping down sideways sensation. Practice mushing turns by:

1. Starting with a low bank angle and pushing out a little more than you know you should.

2. Allowing recovery by relaxing, centering on the bar, and allowing it to return to trim position.

Purposeful controlled mushing turns can be useful for losing altitude more quickly and with less forward progress over the ground than is the case with coordinated turns.

Diving Turns. Diving turns result in more rapid altitude loss and faster progress over the ground than is the case with coordinated turns. Practice diving turns by:

1. Pulling in and over on the control bar.

2. Returning to center of bar but remaining pulled in once desired bank angle is achieved.

3. Allowing recovery by leveling glider and allowing control bar to return to trim position.

Snap Turns. These are useful for evasive maneuvering and showing off. Carefully practice these with lots of ground clearance in mild conditions by:

1. Pulling in substantially so that a crisp dive is achieved.

2. Rolling the glider. (It will roll quickly!)

3. Pushing out crisply to snap glider around the turn.

You may scare yourself with this one. Work up to it, slowly, and remember you can come back to SLT.

FLYING DOWNWIND

You should, during this stage of your development, become totally comfortable with flying downwind. Start at high altitudes and notice the difference in ground speed between upwind and downwind legs at the same airspeed. You will quickly learn that the glider flies the same into the wind, downwind, and every which way. The goals are not to be freaked out by how fast the ground is going by and to judge airspeed independent of ground speed.

APPROACHES

The figure 8 approach is simple and useful. You should work on perfecting it so that you can land consistently close to where you want to be. One danger with this approach for inexperienced pilots is in the case of a quartering headwind in the LZ.

Figure 31 shows how a pilot can easily put himself in a position where he has to make a downwind turn of nearly 180 degrees just prior to his final approach which will also be a 180-degree turn. That's one too many downwind legs close to the ground.

Therefore you should have another landing approach pattern you can use well. Figure 31 also illustrates the standard aircraft box approach. This pattern, though it requires a downwind leg fairly near the ground is safer than the quartering headwind figure 8 because the pilot has only to perform a 90-degree crosswind turn just prior to his final approach turn which is also only 90 degrees.

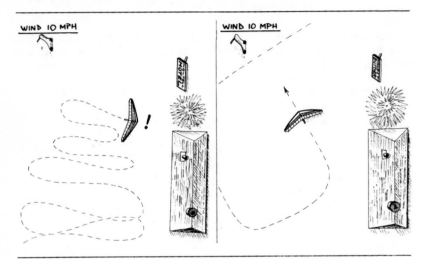

Figure 31. Figure 8 and box pattern approaches.

An extremely important point no matter which approach pattern you use is to **constantly be aware of the location of the LZ and the wind direction in it.** Know where the flag is in any LZ and be sure to look at it several times throughout your approach.

Another skill you should be developing at this stage is the ability to use natural wind indicators in case someone steals the flag in the LZ. The motion of grass, ripples on water, smoke, gliders on the ground, and ground speed reference all reveal wind direction.

ONE LAST THING

The reason you should practice all this stuff in mild, nonlifting conditions is because lifting conditions tend to be either high wind (ridge) or turbulent (thermal). High wind conditions are horribly dangerous for exploring your glider's flight characteristics at different airspeeds and bank angles. Turbulent conditions are horribly dangerous for launching and landing (skills which are not automatic at this stage). Also, you'll have trouble figuring out whether your own tense control input or the rowdy conditions were responsible for putting you weightless in an inadvertent 90-degree wingover.

It should take you a good 5-10 hours of airtime and a good 30-60 altitude flights to master the above described maneuvers and skills. Pick out one or two areas to explore in each flight and I guarantee that by the time you've logged 5-10 hours you'll have learned a lot of useful information about yourself and your glider.

16. Beginning Soaring

In this article we're going to discuss beginning soaring. Nasty old instructor that I am I'm gonna start you off with a multiple choice question. The PRIMARY goal of soaring is:

1. To get as high as possible.

2. To stay up as long as possible.

3. To fly as far as possible.

4. All of the above.

5. Some of the above.

6. None of the above.

Congratulations to those of you who answered 6 (none of the above). Odds are you'll live long healthy lives and be great successes at whatever you do forever. To those of you who gave any other answer I can only recommend that you buy lots of life insurance, draw up a comprehensive will immediately, and prepare to meet your maker.

Listen. The PRIMARY goal of soaring, sledding, training, even ground handling, is to get it done SAFELY. If you ever forget that SAFETY is the main consideration for any form of flying you immediately become the proverbial "accident waiting to happen," a regular card carrying member of FBRMOW (Future Big Red Messes of the World).

No doubt about it, soaring in a hang glider is exhilarating beyond belief, especially if you're just getting into it. It's also dangerous beyond belief if you let the exhilaration you feel evict SAFETY from first place on your list of priorities.

With that perspective welded to our hearts and minds let's go ahead and take a look at what it takes to

— TA DA —
SOAR, BABY!!

THE CATERPILLAR ANALOGY

Here's how a caterpillar becomes a butterfly: First, he finds a spot where he's comfortable and decides to stay there for a while. Next, he gets all wrapped up in a cocoon and proceeds to undergo some major changes. During all this, he retains the shape and limitations of a caterpillar. Finally, after weeks and weeks of the same old stuff (metamorphosis has got to be tedious as all get out) he sheds the cocoon and finds himself with a brand spanking new set of WET WINGS!! What on Earth is he gonna do with WET WINGS? Since brand new butterflies are programmed to hang out at the same old spot until their wings dry out, that's exactly what they do. You will NEVER see a wild-eyed butterfly plummet from a tree because he tried to take off before his wings dried out.

Since us humans are too smart to be programmed in the same sense as the butterfly we retain the wet wing plummet option. Humans who fly hang gliders have been known to exercise the plummet option by going out to some small ridge in high winds and trying to SOAR before their wings are dry behind the ears.

WHAT THE HELL I'M TALKING ABOUT

Uhhh — let's see — Oh yeah! Beginning soaring. The point I'm trying to make is this: There is a good chance you will appear to yourself as being ready to soar before you actually are. The two main elements to that statement are "Ready" and "Soar," and if I ever hope to get anywhere with this discussion I guess I'm going to have to define both.

READY?

Your readiness to soar is a function of your skill mastery level and the range of conditions you are comfortable launching in, flying in, and landing in. When we're talking skill mastery, we're talking absolute mastery of all Novice level skills and significant progress toward mastery of the following Intermediate level skills (quoting from USHGA Pilot Proficiency Rating System):

Section 8: Must show thorough pre-flight of harness, glider, and parachute.

Section 9:   With each flight, demonstrates method of confirming hook-in just prior to launch.

Section 10:   All takeoffs should be aggressive, confident, and with a smooth transition from running to flying. (Slow, unstable launches are double deadly in conditions strong enough to be soarable.)

Section 11:   All landings must be safe, smooth, and controlled.

Section 12:   Demonstrates ability to differentiate airspeed from ground speed.

Section 13:   Demonstrates linked 180's along a pre-determined ground track showing smooth, controlled reversals and proper coordination at various speeds and angles of bank.

Section 14:   Can explain stall warning characteristics of glider.

Section 15:   Has practiced and can demonstrate gentle stalls and proper recovery. Stall manuever to be initiated with no less than 500' ground clearance.

Section 16:   In 8-15 mph wind demonstrates ability to maintain airspeed at or near minimum sink during cross wind or upwind legs without any evidence of stalling.

Section 18:   Demonstrates proper airspeed control on landing approach when descending through a gradient.

Section 19:   Demonstrates proper airspeed for maximum distance (progress over ground) flown into a significant headwind.

As I stated in article 15, it is my view that mastery of skills required for soaring flight can only be achieved through a minimum of 5-10 hours airtime in sled ride or extended sled ride conditions. (No stronger than you trained in.)

When we're talking range of conditions you are comfortable with, remember this: The flying around part of hang gliding is easy and relatively risk free compared to the taking off and landing parts. You don't want to RISK a takeoff or potential landing in conditions that are too strong in reference to your takeoff and landing skills.

Last year an inexperienced pilot in my area had a fatal accident as a result of stalling a takeoff in gusty, high wind conditions that he had no business even setting up in. Why did he do it? He knew he was good enough to handle the conditions once airborne but he chose to ignore his glaring deficiencies in the area of launch skills.

Once again, there are three basic skill areas: Launch, Flying Around, and Landing. Your decision to fly should be based on the limitations of your WEAKEST area.

Look at soaring this way. You can only soar when conditions are moderate to strong. This means higher wind velocities and/or more turbulence. Be like the caterpillar and stick with sled rides or extended sled rides until you're well on your way to mastering the skills listed above. You will then have your wings. Dry those puppies out by gradually expanding the range of conditions you can handle. Before you know it you will be able to:

SOAR!!

I've come to the conclusion that a pilot whose skill and range of condition progression has been safe and gradual will figuratively stumble into his first soaring flights. I mean, that's how it happened with me!!! It must be right!?

Here's how it happens: Through practicing the manuevers I outlined for you in article 15 (in sled ride conditions) your skill level increases. Your increasing skill level allows you to comfortably take off, fly around, and land in progressively stronger conditions. This gives you incrementally more airtime per flight and more time to get wired to your glider's low speed flight characteristics. Simultaneously you get progressively more confident in your ability to control your glider smoothly and quickly. This enables you to turn comfortably just a little closer to terrain where lifting air tends to hang out.

Since soaring is nothing more than flying around as slow as you safely can in lifting air, all of a sudden you find yourself flying around ABOVE TAKEOFF and howling ecstatically.

You are, yes indeed, finally SOARING. Congratulations!

HOT AIR

Now let's look at the real challenge to beginning soaring pilots: sorting through all the nonsense terminology that experienced pilots use for the direct purpose of intimidating new pilots. I know when I was just beginning to soar I was totally intimidated by loud conversa-

---

tions among grizzled veteran sky jockeys who took turns inundating one another with absolutely amazing descriptions of what they "got up in."

There was "Dynamic Ridge Waving," "Lenticular Street Sucking," "Alto Convergence Shear Zoning," and the one I thought might be a fib, "Intergalactic Beam Tracking." I spent a good deal of time wallowing in feelings of inadequacy because all I was doing was trying desperately to stay in your more pedestrian "Ridge Lift" and/or trying to stumble across your average small piece of "Thermal Lift."

Well I'll be damned if I didn't soon discover that most of these grizzled veteran sky jockeys were more or less vying for the Post Diving, Paul Bunyan, Tall Tale award. The only difference between me and them was they got bored quicker talking about your average thermal so they'd start talking about getting caught up in a "Cumulo Resonant Air Temblor" or gaining 200' in a gopher fart instead.

Believe me, most other pilots are out there doing what you're trying to do and that is work some combination of good old down home ridge or thermal lift.

DOWN HOME RIDGE LIFT

Hypothetical pure ridge lift has the following advantages and disadvantages for beginning soaring pilots:

Wind (+) Generally smoother than that associated with thermal lift.

(-) Higher velocity necessary to create lift.

Proximity to Terrain (+) Area of lift well defined and consistent in relation to terrain.

(-) Area of lift gets progressively closer to terrain as wind velocity decreases. Temptation to work too close in "marginal" conditions.

Takeoff (+) Piece of cake to launch in smooth, moderate to high winds.

(-) Launch area is generally steep or cliff. Little margin for error.

Landing	(+)	Piece of cake to land in smooth, moderate to high winds.
	(-)	Must beware of rotors if landing is on top. Penetration out to a landing area may be a problem once lift is left. (Laminar head wind.)
Working Lift	(+)	Good place to master turns of up to 180 degrees. Good place to learn where minimum sink lives on your control bar.
	(-)	Bad place to practice 360-degree turns due to excessive ground travel during downwind leg.
Traffic	(+)	Predictable patterns if everyone follows rules.
	(-)	Area of lift is limited, can get real crowded real quick as breeze diminishes.

YOUR AVERAGE THERMAL LIFT

Hypothetical pure thermal lift has the following advantages and disadvantages compared to ridge lift:

Wind	(+)	Lift can be present even if wind velocity at takeoff is very low.
	(-)	Generally more gusty and switchy as thermals cycle through. Must take into account gust and switch factor as well as peak velocity.
Proximity to Terrain	(+)	Frequent opportunity to encounter large, smooth areas of lift well away from terrain.
	(-)	Temptation to work small, turbulent areas of lift close to terrain. Beginning soaring pilots have no business scratching around near ridges in search of thermals. See (-) under "Working Lift" heading.

Takeoff   (+) Generally sloping terrain and lower wind velocities. More margin for error.

(-) Must watch out for gusts, lulls, switches, etc. Must be prepared to run hard at all times.

Landing   (!) No pros or cons here. Terrain and conditions will vary a great deal. Scout the landing area every time you fly.

Working Lift (+) Once well away from terrain, good opportunity to practice 360-degree turns, reversals, turns with induced yaw, etc.

(-) Thermal lift, by definition, occurs in turbulent air. Areas of sink as well as lift. It is difficult for beginners to tell whether conditions or control inputs are responsible for climbing, sinking out, or getting thrown around.

Traffic   (+) Good opportunity for wide spread of traffic when conditions are moderate to strong.

(-) Working the same thermals with others can be dangerous. Turbulent air can cause changes in heading so traffic patterns are not entirely predictable. Rules of thermaling and thermaling etiquette are more complicated than rules of the ridge.

SUMMARY

Don't try to soar before you're ready. In fact, don't TRY to soar at all. Just keep practicing and getting better and before you know it your increasing skill level and your increasing range of suitable conditions will conspire to hurl you majestically above takeoff. When you finish howling ecstatically, take the time to be proud of yourself. As the stately old actor John Houseman might say: You EAAAARNED IT !!

17. Beginning Cross Country Madness

So I gotta tell you this. After completing the article on beginning soaring (Article 16) I was commencing to feel pretty smug. I've been getting a lot of positive feedback about the column from a variety of sources. Instructors, students, lone wolf pilots, my Mom, and my girlfriend have all been telling me what a good boy I've been for bringing "The Right Stuff" to you each and every month. Apparently, you folks are finding my articles informative, entertaining, and (gasp) useful. So naturally I let it all go to my head (raised nose angle) and feet (fixed struts) whereupon I became a prime candidate for ICIS (Instructional Columnist's Intermediate Syndrome). Fortunately one day while I was pirouetting around in search of yet another topic to provide enlightenment on, I stumbled across a profound truth and was thereby saved from falling prey to the dreaded ICIS.

The truth is this: My articles are at best useless and at worst dangerous UNLESS they are used in conjunction with, or subsequent to completion of, a competent training program. The image of someone out there surrounded by "Right Stuff" articles, trying to teach himself to fly, scares me to death. I sincerely thank the guy who brought that grisly image to my mind by telling me how all the people he works with fly and how they can't wait for him to get his magazine so they can read "The Right Stuff" and learn to fly better. Once again, the only safe way to learn to fly is to get involved in a competent training program. Written material should be used only to fill in the gaps and to augment the learning that takes place, in person, under professional supervision.

Now that I've got that ton of bricks off my chest, I've decided to take a break from preaching the conservative ethic and the spirit of safety. No "be careful" admonishments this time. THIS time I'm going to relate to you my very own personal experience at BEGINNING CROSS COUNTRY SOARING. It's a hair-raising tale of intrigue, suspense, comraderie, and the ability of a tummy ache to render ludicrous the entire concept of Man's Indomitable Will.

I've noticed that all articles about cross country flying start out by "setting the scene, meteorologically speaking." Not wanting to appear too much the Rube, despite the fact that I'm talking about my very first XC flight, I've decided to follow suit.

HOW COLD IT WUZ THE NIGHT BEFORE

Enter Mark Bennett. UP dealer rep, XC expert, young punk, and a man I call friend. We had decided weeks ago to go flying together. After the flight Mark and I convinced ourselves that down deep, in the basements of our hearts, we knew all along it was gonna a "super-bitchin' day." The following conversation reveals what we really knew on that fateful day. Site: Cucamonga LZ.

Mark: Ya think it's gonna be cold?
Erik: I dunno, why?
Mark: I was real cold last night.
Erik: Seems kinda hot right now.
Mark: Yeah — I don't get it.
Erik: Me neither. You got sum gloves I kin borrow?
Mark: Uh Huh. But they don't got no fingers.
Erik: That's OK. It's pretty hot.
Mark: Yeah — I don't get it. Last night I was reaaal cold!
Erik: How cold?
Mark: Well, I had my best jammies on, and my gurl was with me, and I had my waterbed on "steam" and I wuz still cold. You got sum shoes I can borrow? All I got is my flip-flops.
Erik: Yuh. I got sum shoes. It's hot now, though.
Mark: Yuh. Let's go up there.
Erik: OK. Let's go.

Like I said, we could feel it in our bones. We knew we could achieve altitude gains of 6,000' to 7,000'. How'd we know? Simple. We did a quick calculation of the AM/PM temperature differential, determined the lapse rate, adjusted for atmospheric moisture content, and went for it, knowing full well that we were embarking on a cross country flight of major significance.

I wasn't man enough to admit this to Mark but I was real glad I didn't see no gust fronts morphologizing out there as they usually indicate the presence of those atmospheric dreadnaughts I been readin' about.

Anyway, you get the picture. Two jaded Southern Cal pilots who are used to falling out of bed into a big grinning thermal and finding out just how stupendous the day is on their way to the ionosphere. I liked the way Mark put it when he said: "Conditions?? — I don't evaluates 'em, I just flies in 'em!!"

OUR GANG

Spanky, Alfalfa, Buckwheat, and Wheezer. I guess I get to be Wheezer owing to my advanced years and general physical condition. I like Mark as Spanky. If you knew the other pilot in our group, Chuck (Hot Licks) Hicks, you'd probably like him as Buckwheat. That leaves Alfalfa to our illustrious driver, a long tall Texan named John (Yessirree) Shook. I consider John one of my best students despite the fact that he is essentially a human analogy to a Gatling Gun and "Wuffo" questions are his bullets. We nearly had him convinced that it was customary for a driver to pay us pilots ten bucks for the privilege of driving for us. Chuck wanted him to put gas in his 4WD pickup as well but in the end we let poor John off cheap — he got to buy us a six pack.

THERE I WAS

Cucamonga LZ is 2,000' ASL. Launch is at 4,800' and the peak is at 9,200'. Getting from 2,000' to 4,800' is a cinch for me and Spanky. We ride in the back of the truck and tell dumb jokes. Buckwheat has a much tougher time. He rides up front with Alfalfa who, as is his habit, rains a hail of woofos and whyfos all over po' Buckwheat's head.

About half way up we see a glider take off. By the time we get to launch he is well over the peak and climbing. It suddenly dawns on me that my manhood is at stake. I mean, THERE I WAS, with Spanky, one of the best XC pilots in the whole world, at a great XC site, in perfect XC conditions, with visions of Pinecrest Airpark (18 miles) and even Palm Springs (50 miles) dancing in my head. I set up as quickly as my trembling hands will allow, give a bewildered Alfalfa Andy Jackson's number at Pinecrest, put on my fingerless gloves, and dive off.

So now I'm out there in the blue, thrashing around in search of that big grinning thermal I told you about earlier. I'm flying Gene (General Blight) Blythe's personal glider for the first time and quickly discover that The General likes his glider trimmed slower than I'm used to so now I'm all set up with plenty of good excuses if I blow it and go down instead of the preferred UP.

I'm well on my way to having to use these excuses when I run into a thermal that I can't fight my way out of. Salvation!! Two hundred feet back up the hill at launch I can almost hear Alfalfa tell Buckwheat and Spanky that Wheezer has finally gotten his glider out of plummet mode and is now being hurled peakward by a force obviously beyond his control. Spanky, who has never flown Cucamonga before, figures it's safe to launch now that I've shown him all the places where lift isn't. Spanky flies into the thermal I'm caught up in and proceeds to show me where the top of it is. I quickly evaluate the evidence and determine that Spanky is simply a young punk showing off. To hell with him, I say, I'll find a bigger, better one which I promptly proceed to do. Spanky follows me and shows me the top of that one too. Damned kids!

WILD MANZANITA BUSH

About this time I look down and see Buckwheat's glider pointed the wrong way about 30' below launch. I figure that he blew his launch but later he tells me that, in the middle of his takeoff run, a wild manzanita bush let out a blood curdling yell, leaped six feet in the air, and grabbed his left tip. He had no choice but to fly right back at it and kill it with his downtube so it wouldn't hassle anyone else ever again. Alfalfa, who got to calm the indignant Buckwheat down, later corroborates the story while Buckwheat stands behind him slapping half a downtube against his open palm.

MEANWHILE, BACK IN THE SKY, WHEEZER AND SPANKY

Continuing our little game, I keep showing Spanky the bottoms of big grinning thermals and he keeps showing me the tops. The thermals are starting to act like drunks at a square dance. Charlie Daniels is playing "Throw Your Partner to the Peak" on his electric fiddle, I'm spinning off 360's down around the drunks' hob-nailed boots trying to keep from getting stepped on, and Spanky, making like a gnat, is buzzing around their ears.

Right about Peak level, one of the more energetic drunks leans down, inserts the first two fingers of his hairy hand into my nostrils, lets out a rebel yell, and hurls me upward at a speed that threatens to break my poor confused vario. I'm somewhere between terrified and elated as a result of this turn of events. Terror wins out when the Rebel's big brother, hanging out at 11,000', decides I've had enough fun and says so by slapping down hard on the top of my diver. I take this as a signal to leave the party and head for Pinecrest. Meanwhile, Spanky tops out at about 12,000' and takes a tour of a few ski resorts to the West before joining me on my flight (as in Flee) to Andy Jackson's trailer at Pinecrest.

So now that I'm not getting pummeled by the drunks, I have time to become aware of the finger pops at the end of my hands. I think of Spanky's words at the LZ ("I was reaaal cold") and swear I'll never leave my own gloves out of my harness bag again. I decide there is nothing I can do about being cold so I force myself to do something useful. The only thing I can think to do is PANIC about my chances of making Andy's so I do that.

MAKING IT

To make a long story short, my "concern" about making it to Andy's is ridiculous. I get there with 2,000' to spare just as a shear is moving through. Substantial lift is everywhere and visions of Palm Springs, maybe even — DETROIT! burst into my brain. Simultaneously, a clear wave of nausea bursts into my belly. Airsick? With Palm Springs and Motown just a few short miles to the East? I weigh the prospects of blowing lunch in midair against the prospects of having dinner with The Supremes and decide: to heck with The Supremes. I WANNA LAND RIGHT NOW!

So once again, there I am — fighting my way down through lift a pilot dreams about. About 300' off the deck, I'm stuck in lift so I do what I can. I start screaming for someone to throw up dust because I don't believe what I see. There is no wind at Andy's. Now I've landed at Andy's in every condition imaginable but never in conditions like this: stuck in lift 300' off the deck and NO WIND? Andy and Steve Corbin throw dust and wonder who the hell is coming in and why they want dust when there are two perfectly good flags in plain sight. I land, unhook, lie down for a minute, then amble over to Steve and Andy to get the guffaws taken care of. By and by Spanky cruises in and I, having conquered my tummy ache, swagger over like an XC veteran to effuse about my very first, TADA, XC flight. I fess up to a "mild" case of nausea but leave out the part about my ill-fated date with Diana Ross.

THE LEGEND

Buckwheat and Alfalfa dutifully come pick us up. Buckwheat is a little on the somber side. We all cheer him up by telling him what a good guy he is for killing that vicious manzanita bush. He proves he's OK by stoically suffering through the usual blow by blow description of our quest into the unknown. Alfalfa is strangely quiet because he can't believe that his very own instructor, whom he looks up to and admires, has just now, after six YEARS of flying, gotten around to flying somewhere other than the designated LZ. HE wants to do it tomorrow!

We all pile into Buckwheat's truck and head for the obligatory pizza-beer joint. As we're pulling out Andy and Steve Corbin are standing next to each other laughing. I know what they're saying, the heartless creeps. They're saying "There goes Airsick Fear. He spits up an edition of 'The Right Chunks' each and every month. Now he's an XC pilot, winner of the coveted UP 18.235 mile T-shirt [Figure 32], a legend in his own mind!"

Figure 32. Airsick Fear receives his 18.325 mile T-shirt.

18. Doo Dah Days

In this article I'm going to yammer on about an essential piece of hang gliding's socio-cultural matrix, namely the "Doo Dah Day." For those of you who don't know from no "Doo Dah Day," let me define it as: The day that you just gotta satiate your passion for flying hang gliders but can't because Ma Nature is acting like a fool and dealing out hurricanes or low clouds or anything else that shuts down all your flying sites. When you can't fly, but you gotta do SOMETHING that has SOMETHING to do with flying, or reminds you of flying, what you got on your hands is a big Triple D.

Anyone who flies hang gliders is at least familiar with the "Doo Dah Day." We all have them, especially in the winter. There exists, however, a gang of pilots on the East Coast to whom the Doo Dah Day is a way of life. While I was home for Christmas I stumbled across this group and was mightily impressed.

What follows is a heart warming (I'm serious, dammit!) story about the people of the Capitol Hang Gliding Association (D.C. area) and the Maryland Hang Gliding Association (Baltimore area). It's a story about courage and charisma, and the joyful stoicism of a group of pilots who get shut out of flying on a regular basis. It's about the way they cope and preserve and sustain a rollicking community of pilots who are, of necessity, utterly devoted to each other and to the image as well as the act of flying hang gliders.

They go way, way back.

ROOTS

Fade in. It's de dead of wintuh in de Washington D.C. area in the year 1772. De CHGA is habbin' its annual Christmas party at de local pub and house of magic in Chevy Chase, Maryland. All de mens and womens (no chilluns) are gathered around a solitary minstrel. Sad eyes and shufflin' feet everywhere as the minstrel strums his banjo and all join in a bluesy rendition of:

Wintuhtiiiiiiime
An' de flyin' ain't easy
Fronts is gustin'
An' de clouds is way low.

Snow's a flyin'
Or the rain is a freezin'
I done been hang dribin'
Fo' six months or mo!

Eyes sparkle, feets start a tappin', and the minstrel, a shortish, roundish gennelman with a dark moustache and a mischievious, somewhat evil smile, picks up on the mood. He slaps his banjo and pretty soon all de mens and womens are jumpin' and grinnin' and singin':

Gonna hang drive all day
Gonna hang drink all night
Bet my money on a nice cold front
But de hail stones guv me a fright.

And the party rocks on 'til the wee hours or: "All the Doo Dah Day." Fade out.

HANG GLIDERS JOIN THE CHGA

And so it went for two centuries until 1972 when the CHGA's resident grandaddy, Les (Pappy) King, discovered that hang gliders had finally been invented. Les was so excited about the possibility of flight in the capitol area that he ran out and bought two (count 'em, two) hang gliders. He showed one to the only living descendent of the minstrel, a shortish, roundish mustachioed gentleman who had inherited his quadruple great grandaddy's expression of benign mischief. Wojo, as this man was called, went wild upon seeing Les' new toys. He immediately threatened Les with $400.00 and the first retail sale of a hang glider in the D.C. area was thereby consummated.

Though Les had never sold a hang glider before, he knew enough to insist on test flying the contraption prior to delivery. Leaving his own glider at the base of the test fly site, Les walked Wojo's wing to the top, strode off into the blue, and landed smack dab on top of his own glider, totaling both.

The two friends had enough sense to laugh the whole incident off, though Wojo did insist that Les shed the nickname "Pappy" and adopt the more appropriate moniker "Crash." (This was later amended to "Splash" but that's another story.) That settled, the two decided to get on with the business of introducing hang gliders to the rest of their friends in the CHGA.

Joe (Phoebe) Davis, Bob (Albino Rhino) Lowe, Jim (Troll) Gilday, and Ron (Say Hey) Bynaker all had reactions similar to Wojo's which is to say they all bought gliders and proceeded to thrash about the area in search of airtime.

What they found out is this: Flying in the D.C. area is absolutely **righteous** when it's right. Stumble upon the right conditions at High Rock in the Catoctin Mountains and you can fly 47 miles back to Gaithersburg like Bob (The Coach) Deffenbaugh did some time back. Trouble is it's only right once in a blue moon and it's extremely difficult to accurately predict when it's going to be right. End result? An entire flying community knee deep in "Doo Dah Days" with only the glimmer of a faint hope of an occasional righteous day and, of course, themselves.

A RECENT CHRISTMAS PARTY

Fade in. E. Fair, D.C. home boy and legend in his spare time, enters the Brookfarm Inn of Magic where the CHGA is holding its annual Christmas Party. The bar is filled with friendly animated people, many of whom are extremely pretty ladies. A good many of these ladies are wearing blue long sleeved T-shirts with "Wojo's Angels" emblazoned across the front.

Fair, who knows nothing of the CHGA at this point in time, suspects he has discovered the first hang gliding harem and immediately ferrets out the shortish, roundish, etc. Wojo to demand to be let in on his secret. Wojo just smiles which sets Fair, a superficial Californian, to guessing. "Is it money?," says Fair taking one DeLorean approach. Silence. "Is it drugs?," says Fair taking the other DeLorean approach. No response. Fair switches to the Valley Girl approach and wonders aloud if Wojo is "totally awesome" with regard to physical endowment. "Don't be ridiculous," says Wojo before dismissing Fair as a hopeless nincompoop.

Fair wanders around the party for several hours. He meets dozens of men and women, none of whom have had an hour of airtime in the last three months and all of whom are having a great time just being with each other. Fair decides to investigate the matter of the CHGA. He wants to know how they keep their spirits high despite the overwhelming odds against them. Fade out.

BOB & MARGO HELP PROVIDE SOME ANSWERS

Bob Deffenbaugh and Margo Daniels, owners of the D.C. area's primary hang gliding shop, Sport Flight (Gaithersburg, Maryland), helped me sort the whole thing out over dinner one night. It's like this:

In certain areas all year round, and in most areas for certain parts of the year, bad weather greatly diminishes and sometimes eliminates a hang glider pilot's chances of getting airtime. That fact can be depressing, or it can be tolerable, or it can even be enjoyable from a social standpoint. It all depends on how you as a individual pilot and your area's community of pilots go about handling the "Doo Dah Day." One option, of course, it to sulk and grouse and sell your stinking hang glider and take up bowling.

Another option is to develop an individual attitude of stoic acceptance coupled with creative thinking as to alternative activities which can be enjoyed on fogged-in hillsides or cold mountain tops, in winds gusting to 50 mph or blowing down 5 mph. Hackey sacks, frisbees, footballs, R.C. airplanes, on-site manufactured paper and styrofoam airplanes, all have their places in your average DDD.

When you know the odds are bad, look at "hang driving" as "touring the countryside." Take your glider along for the exercise of loading and unloading it and to be prepared for the possibility of an "emergency" (unexpected flyable conditions).

When you set out on a marginal day set out with the idea of having fun whether it involves flying your glider or not. Another option, if you're in an area like the D.C. area that has a strong, supportive flying community, is to take advantage of that community. Hang around the shops. Involve yourself in impromptu seminars on tree landings, parachutes, emergency gear, glider maintenance and repair, etc. Group "moan-ins" about the weather are fun too. Plan an event or tell stories. Use those Doo Dah Days to **socialize**, brother, because you can't socialize in midair underneath a hang glider.

I guess that's what struck me so intensely about the CHGA and the MHGA. The folks have figured out how to ENJOY, not just tolerate, the Doo Dah Day. I think they have something there.

P.S. The CHGA has the highest percentage of women members of any USHGA chapter and if THAT isn't a measure of their success as a hang gliding organization, I don't know what is. That of course means that Wojo doesn't have any secrets. He's just a nice guy who has a soft spot in his heart for women hang glider pilots and they return the favor by having a soft spot in their hearts for him.

---

19. Forced Landings

This article addresses the matter of FORCED LANDINGS. I had originally intended to do an article entitled HOW TO POUND A HANG GLIDER first, but in the process of yakking about it with other instructors I came to the conclusion that any article about CRASHING just had to be preceded by an article on how to AVOID crashing.

The best way to avoid crashing, of course, is to not allow oneself to get into a situation where one has to come back to Mother Earth at a time and/or place that is not of one's own choosing. Since few of us are perfect, however, we will from time to time do something stupid or careless and end up staring down the business end of a 12 gauge pine tree or surrounded by leaping manzanita bushes. Blow a launch, grossly misjudge conditions, or scratch too low while trying to work lift and odds are you will be faced with two options: 1) A forced landing. 2) A crash landing.

DEFINITIONS

Crash Landing: A landing, over which the pilot does not or cannot exercise purposeful and effective control, that occurs at a time and/or place that is not of the pilot's choosing.

Forced Landing: A landing, over which the pilot does exercise both purposeful and effective control, that occurs at a time and/or place that is not of the pilot's choosing.

The difference between a forced landing and a crash, then, is precisely the difference between 1) retaining control of your glider and 2) losing or abandoning control of your glider.

By these criteria a forced landing is infinitely preferable to a crash landing, assuming those are your only two choices. In this article we'll look at the theory and execution of forced landings. After you've all had a while to mull over what it will take for you to maximize your ability to execute a forced landing (thereby avoiding a crash landing), we'll get into the theory and execution of crash landings.

THE DIFFERENCE BETWEEN FL'S AND RL'S

Forced Landings are definitely more difficult to perform than Regular Landings. They generally involve fewer, less desirable options, and little or no time to think. Reactions must be immediate and correct. The terrain is, by definition, at least unfamiliar and possibly totally foreign to one's experience. As if that weren't enough, FEAR of the unknown and FEAR of injury generally compete to take over your mind and body and thereby force you to relinquish control of your glider to a greater power.

Your auto pilot, which is based on experience and instinct, is in charge of forced landings. If your auto pilot is likely to seize up at the prospect of anything other than a "normal" landing, you and he are both going to be in deep trouble someday when your life depends on his ability to put a glider down between two trees on a 45 degree slope. It behooves you to do everything you can to supply your auto pilot with the experience and cultivated instinct necessary to allow him to retain control of your glider during a forced landing.

THE GOAL OF FORCED LANDINGS

The goal of a forced landing is to retain as much control over the glider as possible for as long as possible in order to maximize your chances of putting the glider down wings level at the best possible location at the lowest possible ground speed. The ability to achieve this goal varies greatly from pilot to pilot and involves a working knowledge of the dynamic interrelationship of the following variables:

airspeed	obstacles
glide slope	sink rate
slope of terrain	altitude
control authority	wind speed and direction
body position	

The better able you are to RECOGNIZE the interrelationships of these variables and instinctively MANIPULATE them to meet your needs, the better chance you have of pulling off a successful forced landing. It also helps a lot if you know from personal experience how a well-executed landing FLARE can save you when all seems lost.

Let's look at some of these variables in various convenient clusters.

BODY POSITION / CONTROL AUTHORITY / FLARE

A forced landing is like any other landing in the sense that you should always try to land on your feet, and your feet should always be ready to RUN out of the landing if neccessary. Birds never land head first; neither should you. Also if you've flared a little late, or not enough, you can run out the landing. If you've flared a little early, you can hold the flare and land on your feet, using your legs as shock absorbers. Your legs make better shock absorbers than your head.

For all but the most primitive gliders your hands should be on the downtubes throughout the landing sequence. Where they should be on the downtubes is a matter of personal taste though you should be aware that you need to strike a balance between pitch leverage and roll leverage.

Generally speaking, the higher you place your hands on the downtubes the more pitch authority and the less roll authority you achieve. If your hands are too high you'll be able to flare like nobody's business but you'll have a heck of a time keeping your glider level. Conversely, if you keep your hands too low, you'll be able to roll like nobody's business but you'll have difficulty achieving a full effective flare.

Practice the basic landing position (Figure 33) in midair (calm conditions, well away from terrain) until you find the right position for you. REMEMBER, always have your legs available to run and find a hand position that gives you a good blend of pitch and roll authority at low airspeeds.

Figure 33: Basic landing position.

AIRSPEED / CONTROL AUTHORITY

You should be thoroughly familiar with how quickly and how much your glider responds in pitch and roll over a wide range of airspeeds. You should be absolutely wired to the variations in control authority at various airspeeds while in your basic landing position. Fly fast in this position and fly slow in this position. Note at various airspeeds the differences in sound and feel (control pressures and air in face). Take special care to tune into the fact that at progressively lower airspeeds your glider will become progressively more difficult to roll.

Do the following exercise in calm conditions with at least 500' ground clearance:

1. Assume basic landing position.

2. Pretend you are landing. Gradually slow down from best glide to stall while maintaining wings level. <u>Do not flare.</u>

Your increased experience in the basic landing position over a wide range of airspeeds, will enable you to instinctively perform a successful forced landing someday when you need to.

AIRSPEED / SINK RATE / GLIDE SLOPE / FLARE

Again in your basic landing position (high drag position) you need to become aware of how you can vary your rate of vertical descent as well as your horizontal progress over the ground. You need to know from experience that you can lose a fair amount of altitude with relatively little progress over the ground by flying slower than minimum sink in a controlled mush mode without ever experiencing a stall break.

If you did your homework and practiced slowing down while in the landing position in mid-air you will know exactly how much you can deteriorate your glide path (horizontal progress) without losing all roll authority. Use your vario and landmarks on the terrain to help you get wired to your glider's sink rate and glide slope at various airspeeds.

In calm conditions, with 1,000' of ground clearance, slow down to stall (DO NOT FLARE) and see how long you can maintain directional control. Note your sink rate, note what it takes to keep the glider level. Note, if you can, how much altitude you lose during this manuever. If the glider stall breaks, relax and allow it to return to trim speed.

The more ways you learn to vary your vertical descent and horizontal progress while still retaining control of your glider, the more options you will have for performing a successful forced landing.

ALTITUDE / TERRAIN / WIND

For the purposes of this discussion altitude means clearance from obstacles as well as ground clearance, terrain means obstacles as well as slope of, and wind means wind as we know it plus whatever it is that results when otherwise benign air gets messed around by trees, rocks, canyons, and gnarly hillsides.

With regard to altitude it is essential to constantly be aware of how much of it you have left and how much time you have before you will have to deal with an obstacle or the ground. Also, forced landings are considerably more fun if you have the flying skill to conserve and/or lose altitude in a variety of ways.

With regard to obstacles and the ground it is important to remember that, next to those that are capable of killing you outright (like a live wire) the most dangerous obstacles are those that can put you out of control, in a weird attitude, more than 30' off the ground.

Much has been written on tree landings, for instance. The only point I wish to make here is that the better you are at spot landings, the better chance you will have of coming to rest in the warm embrace of a tree that is capable of supporting you and your glider safely above the ground until help arrives. We'll talk about "tripper trees" when we talk about crash landings.

Obstacles should be selected or avoided based on how they rank on the "lethality" scale amongst your list of options.

Regarding slope of terrain and wind I want to offer the following comments. Given no wind to even moderate wind (5-8 mph) it is better to land upslope than downslope, even if it means landing downwind.

Figure 34, following, illustrates this point by showing how a pilot landing upslope has a much better chance, over a wider range of airspeeds, of making his glide path intersect the slope of the terrain (do a landing).

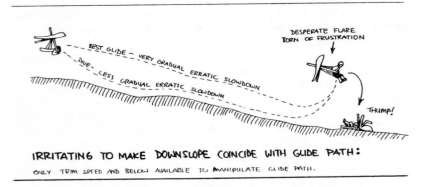

EASY TO MAKE UPSLOPE COINCIDE WITH GLIDE PATH:
GLIDE PATH CAN BE EASILY MANIPULATED OVER A WIDE RANGE OF AIRSPEEDS.

IRRITATING TO MAKE DOWNSLOPE COINCIDE WITH GLIDE PATH:
ONLY TRIM SPEED AND BELOW AVAILABLE TO MANIPULATE GLIDE PATH.

Figure 34: Upslope vs. downslope landings.

Regarding turbulence, wind shadows, and other surprises caused by obstacles and land forms, the only thing I can say is the more experience you have in predicting, recognizing, and dealing with such phenomena the better chance you'll have of successfully performing a forced landing.

FLARE!!!
(Forced Landings Are Really Easy)

Perhaps the best thing you can do to maximize your chances of performing forced landings (or any landings for that matter) is to accept the flare into your heart. The landing flare is your best friend. A well timed and executed flare produces gobs of drag quickly and slows you down dramatically.

A fiercely held flare is good for a straight down, controlled, survivable, vertical descent of 10-30' depending on your skill level, the length of your arms, and your ability to resist the urge to pull back in. You can't do anything about the length of your arms but you can practice flaring at any suitable training hill, so you can directly experience the beauty of the flare and not be afraid of it when it comes time to land in a tight spot.

SUMMARY

Forced landings are more fun than crash landings because you have control over them. Pilots vary greatly in their ability to perform forced, as opposed to crash, landings because pilots vary greatly in their ability to RECOGNIZE and purposefully MANIPULATE the dynamic interrelationships of airspeed, control authority, sink rate, glide slope, body position, terrain, and wind.

A skill essential to the performance of a forced landing is the landing flare. Pilots should be proficient in the timing and performance of landing flares which they should practice at suitable training sites. Pilots should also practice normal flying in their basic landing position in order to familiarize themselves with the sensations and specifics of flying in this position over a wide range of airspeeds up to and including stall.

20. Advanced Pilot Syndrome

Uhhhh ... I don't know exactly how I want to put this. Actually I'd rather not put it any way at all since "IT" is a tremendous source of shame and embarrassment to my favorite pilot (outside of Chuck Yeager) and my favorite author (outside of Kurt Vonnegut Jr.). I am speaking of myself of course and I suspect it's time to stop beating up on the bush and fess up.

The fact is I cannot, in good conscience, pontificate on the subject of crashing as I had hoped to in this article. Remember in Article 19 how I said that any discussion of crashing "just has to be preceded by an article on how to AVOID crashing"? Would you believe: "has to be preceeded by TWO articles on how to avoid crashing"?

Have I said anything yet? No? So imagine a sit-com character, perhaps The Fonz, in that well known situation in which he has to say something that is extremely difficult, if not impossible, for him to say. So imagine ME blue in the face, contorted and struggling, saying to all of you: I BLUUHH, BLUHHHH, ---- I UNGGGHHHHH ---- I BLUUUHH, I (oh Lord save me) BLEW (whew) A LAUNCH!!

Yep. Dead air. The old (treacherous) Mt. Wilson launch site. Me, bloated beyond recognition by holiday turkey and pie, hooked into a 160 sq. ft. glider I've never flown before, having not flown in four weeks, telling myself "Go ahead big fella, you're a pro diver guy, aren't ya?" Ran her right off the hill into some ugly tip snatchin' bushes. Thought I was gonna die. (Walked away without a scratch.) Hand in the cookie jar. Standin' in a corner. Wearin' the dunce cap.

End result? You poor people get to wade through an article on the subject of "Advanced Pilot Syndrome," what it is, how to avoid it, and how avoiding it will keep you from "crashing" which we'll talk about in the next article, assuming I'm not allowed near a hang glider between now and then. Don't go away!! I SWEAR I'll keep the "maudlin confessional" aspects of this piece to an absolute minimum.

WHAT IT IS!!

The way I seized it, Advanced Pilot Syndrome can be defined as: The tendency of a very experienced, thoroughly competent hang glider pilot to take his experience and skills so much for granted that he becomes careless and/or complacent in his observance of safety procedures and in his decision-making processes. (Puff Puff.)

Just so we know who we're talking about let's call "very experienced" 100 hours or more airtime. Let's call "thoroughly competent" achievement of all USHGA Advanced (Hang IV) rating requirements. Anyone who meets either or both of these criteria is a potential victim of the dreaded APS. APS is not to be confused with IS (Intermediate Syndrome) which has been labored upon at length, most recently in article 9. (You Beginner and Novice pilots should be proud of yourselves. You are the only ones in the rating system that haven't had a — Yeccchh — "Syndrome" named after you. Yet.)

WHEN YOU THINK YOU HAVE IT KNOCKED

That, my friend, is when you become extremely vulnerable to APS. It doesn't matter when, where, or who you are. The INSTANT you consider yourself as "having arrived" or as "having everything figured out" is the instant that you become sloppy in your observance of such basic safety procedures as pre-flight checks, hang checks, and regular equipment inspections. Here's how I, an Advanced pilot, know. Within the past six months I have (Yes, this is the "maudlin confessional" part):

1. Failed to pre-flight my glider. (A student was there to take me to task on the matter.)

2. Had to be reminded to hook in just prior to my very first tow launch. And my very second tow launch.

3. Failed to inspect, upon delivery, a new harness and later discovered (subsequent to crash down at Mt. Wilson) that a MAIN support strap had not been sewn together. (The "hot-knifed" connection failed on impact. I had put 10 hours on the harness previously.)

4. Test flown a glider without a #4 batten. (Yes, it had a major league turn in it.)

You wanna talk carelessness and complacency in the judgment department? Look at how much evidence I ignored in the Mt. Wilson debacle. Not only that but I personally know other advanced pilots from all over the country who have in the past year made the following brilliant decisions:

1. Consciously decided not to bother with a hang check for tandem passenger because everything was "just fine last time." (The passenger hung low enough to interfere with the pilot's control.)

2. Initiated a takeoff run in a dead air lull of a downwind day without feeling level and balanced because "I was having trouble getting set and felt I'd be safer in the air." (Stalled, caught tip, crashed.)

3. Initiated a 360-degree turn too low and justified it by "figuring there would be lift (not sink) right next to the ground like there USUALLY is." (Flew into the ground, multiple stitches in the face, badly damaged glider.)

4. Stalled a 180-degree wingover in gusty conditions as a way of celebrating an apparent competition victory. (Fell into glider, deployed chute, landed safely, got disqualified from the meet.)

5. Went for a nostalgia flight on an older, extremely statically tail heavy glider and failed to recognize the need to concentrate on keeping proper angle of attack in the initial few steps of launch. (Stalled launch, caught tip, ground spun back into hill.)

6. Elected to "play around in the bottoms of clouds." (Whited out for 25 minutes, miraculously landed safely.)

7. ETC. and ETC. and on and on ad absurdum.

All perfect examples of Advanced Pilot Syndrome. All results of carelessness or complacency. All performed by pilots who by most standards imaginable are Advanced level pilots with reputations for being conscientious, conservative, and responsible. NO I'M NOT GOING TO NAME THEM. They're all bigger than I am and have fragile egos. (Send $100 to the World Team Fund and I'll send you the names.)

IDIOT LIGHTS

You know those things they put in cars instead of oil pressure gauges, temperature gauges, and voltmeters? Those things that light up red when the car is about to blow up and it's almost too late to do anything about it? Here's some idiot lights that can help you ward off an attack of APS.

1. Yawning during launch. (Advanced boredom.)

2. Leering at girls or boys throughout set-up. (Advanced distractability.)

3. Thinking that this here hang gliding stuff isn't so demanding after all, once you get to a "certain level." (Advanced self assurance.)

4. Shortening or eliminating your pre-flight check. Eliminating your hang check. (Advanced stupidity.)

5. Assuming that favorable conditions and/or perfection in execution of manuevers will see you through questionable situations. (Advanced wishful thinking.)

6. Attempting to do things that you know you really shouldn't be attempting to do just because you "ought" to be able to do them because you are an "Advanced" pilot. (Advanced self delusion.)

7. Forgetting why you're standing around in a cloud on top of a mountain with a 20' long "fat pole" on top of your car. (Advanced senility.)

The point is this: When you see these or other red lights flashing in your face, for God's sake wake up and correct the situation before you crash like me and those other guys did. It's DANGEROUS to feel like you "have it knocked" in this sport. It's even potentially LETHAL. It only takes ONE screw-up to do you in and if you allow yourself to become careless or complacent, no matter how hot you are, you greatly increase your chances of screwing up. You Beginners, Novices, and Intermediates listen up now! You won't EVER "have it made" in this sport and if you EVER think you do you're in a "world of pooh."

DAVE

Since I myself have seen each and every one of the red lights mentioned above since I earned my Advanced rating, and since a few of them have been flashing at me quite recently, I thought — I thought — uhhh — let's see now — what WAS I thinking? Have I said anything yet? Hello? Anyone home? Dave? Is that you, Dave?

21. Crash Landings

Time for a quick and dirty article on the subject of crashing a hang glider. I don't really want to talk about it much and you folks probably don't want to read about it much but it's a subject that bears some looking into. So let's get it bloody well over with shall we?

We've already discussed how to avoid crashing by avoiding the various Syndromes (Intermediate and Advanced) and by practicing manuevers that will increase your ability to perform forced (as opposed to crash) landings. Recall that the difference between forced and crash landings is the difference between retaining control of the glider until "touchdown" and giving up control of the glider at some point prior to "impact."

The main point I wish to make in this article is that the pilot in a crash situation almost always has choices to make that can greatly affect the severity of the consequences of the crash. Choices can and must be made in the following interrelated areas:

1. Point at which control of the glider is abandoned.

2. Positioning of the glider.

3. Positioning of the pilot's body in relation to the glider and terrain.

Choice, of course, implies awareness of options and awareness of options implies control. Crashing, of course, has nothing to do with control, and directly implies being "out of it." Let's start off then with a discussion of the "decision to give up control." (So you can get the freaking crash over with!)

THE DECISION TO ABANDON CONTROL

The main point here is to avoid the temptation to PANIC in a crash situation. The instant you panic is the instant you give up control and if you panic early you are probably giving up many opportunities to substantially improve your situation prior to impact. Retain control of the glider as long as you possibly can. If at all possible retain enough airspeed to level the glider and to execute an effective FLARE just prior to impact. If it is not possible to retain the ability to flare, retain as much control as you can until just before impact when it is time to concern yourself less with control of the glider and more with POSITIONING yourself and your glider so that the glider's frame and your own large boned parts (legs, not head!!) take as much of the impact as possible.

POSITIONING OF THE GLIDER
(Aluminum vs. Bones)

The age old rule for crashing is: Get as much glider as possible between you and the ground just prior to impact. The logic, of course, is to make the GLIDER, not your own precious bod, take the brunt of the crash. Broken aluminum is a lot cheaper and easier to live with than broken bones.

It is my view that the optimum way to crash (if there is such a thing) is rear keel first, followed by control bar. Even if the pilot doesn't let go, as illustrated in Figure 35, Sequence 1, opposite), the control bar and keel take a good deal of the impact without danger of the pilot breaking his arms going through the control bar.

Note also in this sequence how the mid portion of the keel takes impact through the harness after the pilot's legs have buckled (not broken), absorbing shock. A high flare with a 30' rapid vertical descent, then, is better than a high speed nose-in with no flare at all, because the glider and your bod are in a better position to absorb impact.

On nose first landings in which the pilot is unable to stay on his feet and jump through the control bar (thereby preventing or minimizing the nose-in) it is best to let go of the control bar and allow the body to swing through and, hands covering face, arc into the front keel, making it absorb the impact. Another option is to grasp one downtube with both hands so the body will arc to the side. The point here is that a nose plate, control bar landing usually results in the sudden stopping of the glider. Your body will continue into the glider and it is up to you make it do so in a way that is most likely to damage the glider and not your body. Sequence 3 shows a composite of a couple of the classic WRONG ways to position your body on a nose-in crash landing.

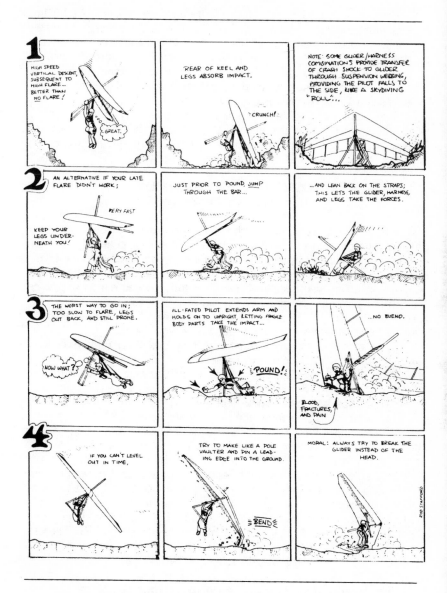

Figure 35: Crash landing sequences.

One more concept regarding positioning the glider to take impact is illustrated in Sequence 4. Here a pilot in the process of crashing off level uses what's left of his pitch and roll authority to pin the leading edge of his glider on the ground and make it absorb the impact of the crash. Had he pushed out hard while continuing a futile attempt to level the glider he would have spun into a high speed downwind nose-in crash with worse consequences.

The point here is there are many creative ways to manuever your glider into taking the impact that would otherwise be reserved for your body. Do what's necessary to break your glider in a crash landing. Your bones will thank you.

POSITIONING OF THE BODY
(Big bones vs. Little bones)

Little bones break easier than big bones and you can run faster on your legs than on your arms. Your head does not generally approve of being crash landed upon. These are very good arguments for trying hard to keep your feet underneath you at all times. It is, in my opinion, an unforgivable sin to crash land fully pushed out in the prone (belly flop) position. No good can come of it. If you don't believe me take another look at Sequence 3 which clearly shows three separate ways a head first nose-in crash can break your body.

First of all if you go through the bar face first, fully extended you're going to want to put one or both arms in front of you to break your fall. What you're actually doing is stiff-arming the ground and it's a great way to break your wrist or forearm. After your arms break your face will hit a rock because you don't have your arms up covering your head and face like you should have.

If you happen to hold on to the downtube as you go head first through the bar, you have a good chance of sustaining a spiral fracture of the upper arm. This is because, as the glider stops abruptly, your body will continue its forward momentum. Since your hand can't come off the downtube due to the presence of your thumb, all that momentum is converted to a torque force on your upper arm. Snapola. Meanwhile your big strong legs are sailing along in mid air behind you doing absolutely nothing for you. (Don't blame them, you put 'em there!)

SO MAKE LIKE A BABY

The fetal position is not a bad body position to assume just before impact. If your legs are underneath you like they should be, and running is no longer going to get you anything, all you have to do is curl them up to your body. Don't suck your thumb, though, as it would look bad. Instead, use your hands and arms to cover your face and head.

NOTE: On a crash that involves a straight down vertical descent, it is best to collapse to one side or the other (parachute landing technique), as in Sequence 1, as this will minimize the chances of spinal injury. On a control bar, noseplate crash, get fetal before the glider hits so you can arc through the control bar.

SUMMARY

Don't crash at all. It's messy and unnecessary. If you're in a crash situation, DON'T PANIC. You may be able to save the situation or at least improve it if you:

1. Retain control of the glider as long as possible.

2. Abandon control of the glider when it becomes more important to get into a position that will allow the glider to take as much of the impact as possible.

3. Keep your legs underneath you because they'll absorb more impact than your arms or head.

4. Get fetal and cover your head just before impact. If you've kept your legs underneath you they will be pushed into a fetal position in the process of absorbing impact.

5. Don't follow rule 4 in the event of a straight down vertical descent. In that case, collapse to one side or the other.

6. Call your mother and tell her you're all right.

22. About Repairs

So ya went and did it anyway, huh? Despite all my bombastic gumbeating about forced landings and crash landings ya had to go out and trash your glider. Now I suppose you're trying to figure out what needs fixing and how to fix it. Well, you're in luck, bunky. This article is going to examine the wreckage of your poor abused glider piece by piece with the intent of giving you some guidelines as to what sorts of dings, gouges, frays, tears, bends, and rebends demand immediate repair or replacement, what sorts demand professional as opposed to home repair/replacement, and what sorts do not compromise the structural integrity of your aircraft and therefore can be lived with.

If perchance you are a member of hang gliding's "distinct minority" and can therefore afford to replace every nicked endcap and every superficially scratched frame component, then you don't need to read this affront to your conscientious thoroughness. Rest assured you are doing things right. Peace of mind alone is a good enough reason for having "Mr. Glidewrench" immediately replace anything on your glider that no longer looks or acts like it did when it was brand new.

No, this article is for those of you whose babies need new shoes, whose rent is due, and whose glider and bank account are either critically damaged or in less than perfect shape. Now I can't say nothin' about nobody's babies or bank accounts but I can help you distinguish between a "critically damaged" and a "less than perfect" hang glider. There is a major difference of course. One can safely fly a less than perfect hang glider but one risks (or automatically forfeits) one's life if one engages in the act of flying a critically damaged hang glider. So if you want to know what sorts of dings demand immediate action and what sorts can be lived with until your next paycheck, read on — you will be immeasurably enriched.

CONTROL BARS

Ah yes, everyone's favorite. The most frequently damaged part on any man's (or woman's) diver. Bend it out, bend it back, eyeball it. Yup. Looks good to me. Before you fall into that trap consider the following facts:

1. The downtubes (uprights, legs, etc.) of your control bar bear a considerable and critical compression load.

2. Any aluminum cylinder that is "out of column" or not perfectly straight is substantially weaker in its ability to bear a compression load than one that is perfectly straight. If you don't believe me get an aluminum can, stand directly on top of it and note that it will bear your weight. While standing on it, bend over carefully and lightly tap the sides with your fingertips. The can, taken out of column by your tap, will immediately collapse under the compression of your weight. (Get your fingers out quick or you'll land on them.)

3. Any time you bend a downtube you cannot possibly bend it back to perfectly straight. Therefore any downtube that has been bent and straightened, even just once, is weaker than one that has never been bent.

4. The longer the downtube, the easier it is to bend it out of col - umn, and the more important that it remain perfectly in column.

5. Aluminum that is bent then straightened is work hardened. That means that the material in the area of the bend is harder but more brittle than it was before. It takes a greater force to bend it again and it's even harder to bend it back to perfectly straight. Repeated bending and rebending of a downtube results in a downtube full of "S" turns.

The message here is: Do not mess around with downtubes. It is an excellent idea to immediately replace one that has been bent at all. It is acceptable to attempt to straighten a downtube that devi - ates less than 2" (along its entire length) from perfectly straight as long as there is no flattening of the tube and no evidence of metal fa - tigue (surface appears hazy in the area of the bend). You can consid- er your attempt to straighten the tube successful if you cannot per- ceive any deviation from column with the naked eye. Straighten it once only.

Basetubes are quite a different story as they bear no critical load and are not in compression. Basetubes can be bent and straight - ened several times, can be scratched and gouged, and can look like a piece of spaghetti. As long as they do not become so deformed that they alter the geometry of the control triangle, and as long as they are there, they're OK. It is a good idea to periodically check a base tube's corner bracket bolt holes for excessive elongation, particularly if the basetube has survived the breakage of several downtubes.

Most control bars aren't real complicated and that's why almost everyone replaces their own downtubes instead of paying "Glidewrench" to do it.

MAIN FRAME COMPONENTS

Keel. There is a good reason for your keel being the wimpiest looking main frame component on your glider. It bears the least load. Yes there is a mild compression load applied by the front to rear wires and perhaps a light bending load if you hang from your keel very far away from the control bar but the main thing a keel does is give glider designers a place to bolt the top of the control bar so it won't fall over. It's also a handy thing to wrap a keel pocket around.

Because the keel is under very little duress in flight you will never hear of a keel failing in flight. Keels get bent and broken all the time on blown landings, however, due to severe bending loads applied either directly (like a vaulting pole) or indirectly via pressure of bodies or other objects on the flying wires.

Because keels bear relatively minor in-flight loads it is quite acceptable to straighten slightly to moderately bent ones, or to cut and splice or sleeve creased or broken ones. It is important to do the job right which means replacing damaged tubing with tubing that is as strong or stronger than the original. It also means getting all the dimensions right and not repairing the keel in a way that puts set screws or rivets under a shear load. If you are reasonably adept with tools and are confident that you can do the job right, go ahead and repair your keel yourself. If you have any doubts, take it to a pro.

Crossbar. Crossbars bear a considerable compression load. Each crossbar half is compressed between its two attachment points: the leading edge and the crossbar center plates of the keel. A column (any member under compression such as a crossbar half) normally fails in the center of the loaded span, which would be the midpoint of the crossbar half. It fails by bowing out of column, and its strength is determined by its stiffness, or resistance to bowing out of column. Since it tends to bow most easily in the middle, that's where stiffness is most important. A designer will sometimes use a sleeve to stiffen the middle of a crossbar half. A sleeve is simply a device to increase wall thickness, and hence stiffness, in part of the tube, and thus can be used to save weight.

You can assume that the designer of your certified glider engineered a crossbar that was strong enough to pass the certification tests. You can't assume that it is necessarily any stronger than that. In other words, you should not assume that it is OK for your crossbar to be weakened by damage, even if only a little bit. The question now is: where and how can a crossbar be damaged and not be weakened? The answer depends on the design of the crossbar, and especially on whether or not the crossbar is sleeved. Consider Figure 36:

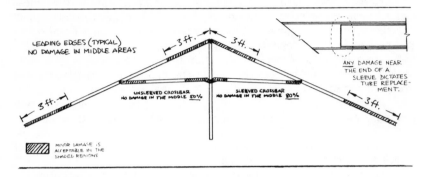

Figure 36. Critical areas of crossbar, leading edge damages.

In an unsleeved crossbar, no damage is permissible within the middle half of the crossbar half. Small dings, dents, scratches, or even a small hole outside of this area will not weaken the column. Any damage, such as a large dent, which changes the alignment of the column is not permissible, because it might introduce an eccentric loading. In a sleeved crossbar, you have to be more conservative. At the end of the sleeve the wall thickness and therefore columnar stiffness changes dramatically. You should therefore not tolerate any damage on a sleeved crossbar that is within the middle 80% of the column.

Generally, crossbars damaged in the critical areas described above should be replaced immediately and not repaired. Also, any device that pins, restrains, or otherwise holds a crossbar into position should be in perfect condition at all times.

It is necessary to remove the sail from the frame to replace the crossbar on some gliders, on others it is not. If you are confident that you can replace the part properly, go ahead. If not, take it to a pro.

Leading Edge. Leading edges are under considerable bending and compression loads. They are almost always sleeved about three feet out from either side of the leading edge, crossbar junction where the bending load is highest. Small surface scratches, and barely perceptible dings or depressions are acceptable along the entire length of a leading edge. Noticeable to moderate depressions, gouges, dings or even small holes within three feet of each end of the L.E. will not compromise its structural integrity if they do not cause a change of alignment of the spar or cause damage to the sail mount points.

It is my opinion that any bent portion of a leading edge, or any leading edge that is significantly damaged in the area shown in Figure 36 should be replaced immediately. It should definitely not be straightened, spliced, or sleeved in any way. Today's gliders feature L.E.'s that are pre-loaded by the sail which means that the bending characteristics of the L.E. are critical to the performance and handling characteristics of the glider. Replacing a leading edge generally, but not always, involves taking the sail off the frame.

RIGGING

Lower Flying Wires. Side flying wires carry almost all of the load in flight. Front to rears, on most gliders, carry almost no load. The main job of front to rear flying wires is to keep your control bar in the same plane. Don't scrimp on side flying wires. Replace them immediately if you have any broken wire strands, kinks, thimble deformity, or any evidence of corrosion or trauma. A tweaked thimble, a kink, or even ONE broken strand can be tolerated for a short time on front to rears. It's not for everyone, you understand, and it's not good practice, but it can be done.

Upper (Ground) Wires. These are not loaded in normal flight but if you get upside down for any reason they're all you've got except for your kingpost which is then required to do the job of two downtubes. You can be forgiven for flying with slightly damaged upper wires, or a slightly out of column kingpost for one or two flights but you're a bad person if you do it more than that.

BATTENS, LUFF LINES, TIPS

Battens, especially preformed ribs, should be in good shape and should basically conform to your batten template. There really is no excuse for flying with broken or seriously deformed ribs because they are easy to straighten and cheap to fix.

Regarding luff lines (or "bridle lines") and fixed tips, assume that both are critical parts of the pitch characteristics of your glider and that both should be at or very close to factory specifications. It is downright dangerous to fly any of today's gliders with damaged or improperly adjusted luff lines or tips. Also, for God's sake, don't follow the advice of guys who say you can lighten your pitch pressure or "make your glider faster" by lowering your luff lines a few inches.

SAIL

Hang glider sails are generally made from resin-stabilized Dacron. Small pin holes and minor wear spots appearing anywhere on the sail except right on the trailing edge are cosmetic nuisances only. Small to moderate rips, tears, or abrasions on or near the leading edges (Mylar, foam pockets) or on the double surface likewise are primarily cosmetic problems. Sticky back Dacron or good old duct tape provide quick, cheap, and dirty solutions to such sail damage.

Rips or tears in the rear body (between double surface and trailing edge) are cause for more concern and should be patched by a professional sailmaker before they get worse. This is especially so if the rip or tear is larger than an inch or two. The reason is this area of the sail, in most gliders, is under a significant amount of tension due to pre-loading of the frame and the stresses of flight.

Small, even miniscule, rips or tears right on the trailing edge (like a split near a batten grommet) are definitely structural hazards and should be fixed immediately. The reason is that the trailing edge is usually under the most tension and there is no surrounding material to take up the slack for the damaged area. The sail then becomes vulnerable to ripping like an old bedsheet.

SUMMARY

If you have the means, by all means replace or repair every part of your glider that sustains damage. If bucks are tight you can fudge a little on the basetube, keel, front-to-rears, and top wires, or on very minor damage to non-critical areas of the crossbar and leading edges as shown in Figure 36. Don't let needed repairs to even these items go undone indefinitely. Only perform repairs or parts replacements that you're absolutely sure you can do right; let a qualified pro do everything else. Don't fudge on side flying wires, downtubes, critical areas of main frame spars, or the trailing edge of the sail.

And FINALLY: Carefully inspect your hang loops for damage or signs of wear each and every time you DON'T FORGET TO HOOK IN. After all, what good is a sound glider if you ain't safely attached to the silly thing?

---

23. Talking Downdrafts With the Pear People

Yeah, well, so here's the deal. We all know there aren't more than two or three bona fide guarantees runnin' around loose on this planet. Death and taxes, of course. Plus the fact that 2 out of 12 people on any given jury panel are complete idiots, seemingly programmed to misinterpret evidence and generally get everything wrong. I always thought that was about all a person could count on. So imagine my surprise when, just the other day, I ran — unsuspecting and headlong — smack dab into an eternal verity of modest but definite proportions.

There I was. The Brea Mall, Brea, California. It was Super Bowl Sunday. I was just standin' out in the middle between The Video Depot and Art's Art shop. To my rear, a pretty little hang glider all set up and shiny. Positioned neatly in front of me, a pile of Hang Flight Systems brochures and other apparati designed to compel passers by to — pause for a moment — then ask thoughtful, intelligent questions about hang gliding in general and my own swell shop in particular. I was, as we say in the trade, "working an action agent oriented, aviation theme Mall Show" in hopes of drumming up some new business.

Ten grueling hours later I realized I had discovered a truth so pure and unwavering, a guarantee so crystalline, that it had to be ranked way ahead of taxes and just behind death on the master list of things a human can count on.

Here it is: Nine out of the ten people who stop at the hang gliding exhibit during a Mall show on Super Bowl Sunday — that's nine out of the ten — will be shaped like a pear and will want to know all about downdrafts. Furthermore, the one out of ten will be whichever of your true blue friends was kind enough to agree to bring you some lunch. It's true — I swear it.

Anyway, as I was standing there jelling on the inside and grinning eagerly on the outside, I had lots of time to refine my responses to the questions presented unto me by the pear people. Any hang gliding Jedi warrior who has spent any time at all attempting to proselytize the general public has his own set of gently reassuring and pleasantly informative dialogue tapes for each of the frequently presented questions. I'm going to share mine with you — yawn — just in case you ever have a chance to use them. May the force be with you.

The good news is that I'm gonna give equal time to The Dark Side and present for your reading pleasure the answers to wuffo questions that I would love to blurt out just once. Just once — to make up for missing Joe (Yoda) Montana's dismantling of the hated Dolphins on that bleak and futile Sunday.

At a distant mall show, not so long ago ——

PEAR PEOPLE

Pears mostly travel in pairs and are easily identified by the shapes of their bodies, as illustrated in Figure 37. Kinda narra' at the shoulder and broad at the hip with varying layers of juicy jiggly tissue masses trowled on in between. Male units usually sport brightly colored wide plaid triple knit pants to accent the port and starboard bulges that would otherwise seem dwarfed by those issuing from the fore and aft mid span. Males are far more verbal than their female counterparts and generally ask all the questions.

Figure 37. Pear people.

Female units done up in rollers and floating freely in their day glow muumuus are usually content to stand beside and slightly behind their mates. In this position the female is at liberty to indulge in free form facial contortions indicating varying degrees and blends of exasperation, martyrdom, and panic as she listens to her mate talk "hand" gliding with some young pup who is obviously bent on separating her male from his money and his life.

The incredible strength of the female pear unit is evidenced by her unfailing ability to "vibe" the male unit the heck out of the mall just after he senses he has "impressed" her with his astute grilling of the young pup and just before he succumbs to his innate desire to "try it just once."

Pears ask questions regarding hang gliding in a fairly predictable sequence commencing with inquiries as to the cost of the inanimate and generally nonthreatening equipment on display and progressing to hushed and timorous wonderings about the evil, unpredictable air masses known to them as "pockets" or "downdrafts."

What follows is a series of typical pear unit questions, more or less in the usual sequence, with "correct" answers followed immediately by those I would like to give ... just once.

RIGS

Like I said, the first questions are about equipment. After all, a hang glider on display poses even less threat to a curious pear person than does a lawnmower in action.

Q: How much does one of them rigs cost?

JW (Jedi Warrior):
> Brand new intermediate level hang gliders, which is what we recommend to our students, range in price from $1,500 to $1,900 depending on the model and the size. You also need a harness, a helmet, and an emergency parachute. Harnesses cost $125 to $300 depending on the type. Helmets range from $40 to $80. Parachutes go for $350 to $425. You can also get good, safe used equipment for one third to two thirds the cost of new equipment depending on availability and the level of performance you desire. If you find equipment available for appreciably less than what I've just indicated, odds are it is outdated and unsafe by today's standards.

DV (Darth Vadar alternative answer):
  Between $50 and $2500. (Pause, appear bored.)

PU (Pear Unit): What's the difference?

DV: Guts. (Inspect fingernails.)

PU: Come again?

DV: Well, a glider is pretty much a glider. They're all worth about $1,500 give or take a hunnert. If you find one for $2,500 it just means that the guy sellin' it has lots of guts to ask that much for it. And, if you find one for $50 the guy sellin' it is probably a gutless, lilylivered puke who's afraid to keep flyin' cuz his mommy thinks he might get killed or somethin' stoopid like that. How much you got, anyway?

Q: How much does that one there weigh?

JW: That one weighs 55 pounds. Modern gliders range from about 50 to nearly 80 pounds depending on the model and size.

DV: Pick it up and see for yerself, fella. If ya break it, it's yers.

Q: Can you still get kits and put 'em together yourself?

JW: Hang glider kits haven't been available for some time due to the fact that the design and fabrication of hang gliders has become a sophisticated and fairly complex process requiring knowledge, skill, and equipment that is unavailable to a vast majority of consumers.

DV: Sure you can get kits. Just be sure to get the "snap together" kind rather than the "glue together" kind. The glue will fry yer brains — if you let it.

GENERALLY SPEAKING

Having exhausted their questions about whatever happens to be in their immediate field of vision, pears typically proceed to general, non-personal questions about the sport and the local terrain where the sport is practiced.

Q: **Where do they Jump from around here?**

JW: (Gives brief description of local flying sites, taking care to use the phrase "fly from" as opposed to "jump off of." Elicits description of what sorts of flying the person has seen, then explains it with ground school type material, i.e.: What you saw was a pilot flying in ridge lift which is caused by blah blah blah.)

DV: Man, we jump off anything we can set up on without gettin' shot at. Most of us carry guns so we can shoot back. Ain't no landowner gonna keep me from flyin'. Say, you live near a hill? Can I land on yer house?

Q: **How safe is hang gliding — really?**

JW: (Shows pear unit Dennis Pagen's article "The Safest Way to Fly?" and John Heiney's "Hang Gliding — A Natural High."

DV: Look, Bud. You want safe you go bowlin'. You want kicks and thrills you go hang glidin'. It's that simple. Now either sign up or get outta here; yer makin' the rest of these suckers jumpy.

HOW ABOUT YOU?

Pears who stick around to emit the next round of questions have generally developed a feeling for the person who is fielding their questions. Pears come up with some very interesting blends of awe, suspicion, envy, pity, and parental concern as their questions begin to reflect a primal and empathetic bonding with this being in front of them who flies like a bird and talks too. Pears want to understand you and help you realize that hang gliding actually is as dangerous as it appears to be to them. Of course, part of them wants to be just like you.

Q: **Don't your arms get tired?**

JW: No, not really. You see, I don't support my weight with my arms. I lie face down in a hammock kind of thing we call a harness. It's attached to the top of the glider at a carefully planned point called the center of gravity. So my body swings like a pendulum inside the control triangle which I grasp with my hands so that I can have leverage to shift my weight around.

DV: Yeah, but I just kind of tough it out.   I figure you only go around once so I'm willing to hang on for dear life and hope that my arms don't get so tired that I'm forced to let go and plunge to my death. So far, so good if you catch my drift.

Q: Can you control those things?

JW: I sure wouldn't have much fun flying hang gliders if I couldn't control them. Actually, I control the glider by shifting my weight around. Since my weight is suspended from the glider's CG, any motion I make will cause the glider to go in the direction of my body weight. If I want to go left, I shift my weight to the left. If I want to go faster, I shift my weight forward and so on. Actually, hang gliders are so controlable that a properly trained pilot flying in reasonable conditions can land on or within a few feet of a bullseye with regularity.

DV: We're not sure but we think so.

PU: You "think" so!?

DV: Well, we mostly all land within a quarter mile of where we think we want to.

PU: Quarter mile!?

DV: (Thinking out loud.) I suppose the wind could be just blowin' us pretty close to where we'd kinda like to be.

PU: The Wind!?

DV: Nah! I'm just kiddin'. The truth is it all depends on your Zoological sign. There are three zoological signs that seem to have more control over their gliders than the rest of us.

PU: (Slyly.) You mean Zodiacal.

DV: Whatever. (Extremely long pause.)

PU: (Exasperated.) Well!?

DV: Well, what?

PU: (Loudly.) What three signs have control over their gliders?!! What sign are you!!??

DV: Don't worry about me bubba, what sign are you?

PU: (Fumbles for ID, finds it, then shrieks.) ARIES! ARIES!

DV: You know, I'm pretty sure that's one of them.

PU: (Whimpering.) Pretty sure!!?? (Passes out.)

Q: Is it scary?

JW: Not if you learn properly and gradually in accordance with a proven USHGA certified instructional program. Better schools structure your learning experience so that there is never a time when you feel ill-equipped to handle the task at hand. For example most schools have you run with the glider on flat ground for a while. This practice teaches you how to do a takeoff run without taking off and also enables you to learn how to stop the glider by doing a landing flare at the end of your "takeoff" run. As your skill level progresses you can avoid being unduly scared by using good judgment and never allowing yourself to get into situations that leave you insufficient margin for error.

DV: (Grinning insanely.) You damn betcha, boy howdy!!!

HOW ABOUT ME?

The more venturesome of the pear units, having gotten this far, will invariably take the next step and make a couple of brazen inquiries as to the particulars of the training program at hand. It is at this point that a Jedi hang glider pilot can look into the eyes of the pear and actually "see" (a la Carlos Castaneda) the pear's image of himself learning to fly a hang glider.

Q: What does it take to learn to fly one of these things? (Or, the sometimes corollary: Do you think I have what it takes to learn to fly one of these?)

JW: It takes motivation more than anything else. You don't have to be particularly brave if you're involved with a competent instructor. If you are in reasonably good health and can run in an average manner, you can learn to fly a hang glider — if you want to. We have some instructional programs for those who are sure they want to fly and others for those who just want to see what it's like. (Describes particulars of the training program in question including opportunities to observe more flying — driving, watching a class at the training hill, etc.)

DV: Son, if you wanna fly these here divergibles you gotta have a whole lot of two things.

PU: Yeah, what's that?

DV: Money and Guts.

PU: Money and "GUTS!!??"

DV: That's right, chump. Give me some money and we'll go out right now to see how many guts you got.

PU: I haven't got the money right now.

DV: Broke and gutless, huh? I guess you're just not cut out to be a diver pilot, Mack.

WHEN THE WIND STOPS

Pears always save their wonderings about downdrafts, air pockets, and wind stoppages until the very end when they know that the panting Jedi is in a weakened condition. Invariably they beat feet after hearing, but not believing, the Jedi's responses to their questions about the air.

Q: How do you guys breathe up there?

JW: We breathe normally. Insofar as the sensation of wind is concerned, flying a hang glider is much like standing on the ground facing into a 25 mph headwind. You feel it on your face and in your hair, but you breathe like you always do. The only exception is that hang glider pilots who fly at very high altitudes sometimes carry oxygen in order to avoid hypoxia. A vast majority of all hang glider flights occur at altitudes where normal breathing works just fine.

DV: The trick is you gotta keep your mouth wide open at all times and fly real fast as much as possible so that your mouth works like a big old ramjet scoop. [See Figure 38.] That's why big mouth guys always seem to fly higher than little mouth guys. They got better air scoops. The other thing is you gotta watch how long you fly around real slow in them thermals. The slower you fly the less "ram" you get in your airscoop. Again, big mouth guys always seem to do better in thermals.

Figure 38. How we breathe up there.

Most of the time we're all havin' too much fun to pay much attention to how high or how slow we're flying so we try to supplement our ramjet air intake by making loud sucking noises in hopes we'll suck in some stray chunks of oxygen.

Did I already mention the fact that the "organic oxygen starvation, brain death syndrome" that most of us experience after a half hour flight is mostly reversible!??

Q: What about downdrafts, air pockets, and wind shears?!

JW: We've all heard about jets and other aircraft having problems with such phenomena so there's no doubt that parcels of radically turbulent air do exist in nature. Radical turbulence, however is generally associated with very strong meteorlogical conditions that no sane hang glider pilot would even set up in. Winds over 25 mph and overdeveloped cloud formations are very visible, easily identified warning signs to hang glider pilots. The point is that hang glider pilots who exercise a reasonable amount of caution, pay attention to the obvious signs around them, and refuse to fly in clearly questionable conditions will never have problems with turbulence of the kind you're asking about.

DV: We don't never worry about them downdrafts or air pockets becuz we know the two are related. Ya see, when an air pocket falls out of the sky it causes a downdraft right under the place it fell out of. It don't matter if we get caught up in the downdraft because once the air pocket hits the ground it becomes a landing cushion so we just land right there, get out from under our gliders, and thank our lucky stars that the wind blowed us over to a safe "air pocket / downdraft / landing cushion zone." We do fret some about wing shears though cuz not one of us knows a thing about 'em.

Q: What do you do when the wind stops?

JW: The wind stopping doesn't cause us any problems. You see, hang gliders aren't dependent on the wind for power. Gravity is what allows hang gliders to fly. The force of gravity causes the glider to move downward through whatever air mass the glider is in and it is this downward motion through the air that enables the glider to fly. You've probably seen hang gliders in the air that are climbing away from the ground. All that means is that the air mass the glider is in is moving away from the ground faster than the glider is moving downward through the air mass. Consequently the glider is going upward in relation to the ground at the same time it is going downward in relation to the air mass.

Since wind flowing up and over a mountain is one of the things that means the air mass is moving away from the ground, once the wind stops, the glider simply flies downward through the stationary air mass until it lands safely on the ground.

DV: There ain't but one thing you can do when the wind stops.

PU: Yeah, what's that?

DV: Plummet, man, Plummet.

THAS' ALL, FOLKS

That's all the drivel I got up my sleeve for this article. Hope you know this is all in good fun. Be nice to the pear units you meet. After all:

Some of them
Will be some of us
One of these
Days
And vice versa.

24. Friends

TWO GUARANTEES

There are at least two guarantees involved in running a retail hang gliding establishment and flight school. One, you AIN'T gonna get rich doin' it. Two, you ARE gonna meet some absolutely fascinating people, some of whom are bound, one way or another, to become your friends.

CAPTAIN COOL SHOES

I first realized how much I liked John P. Rubino when he stopped by my shop one day in dire need of a rest stop. I was out back showing off a glider or something when John sidled up and asked: "Mind if I use your shop to go to the bathroom?" I mumbled something like "Yeah sure, go ahead" and kept doing what I was doing. A few seconds later, from the MIDDLE of my "casually organized" shop, John sings out: "ANY PLACE IN PARTICULAR!?"

Thought I was gonna die laughing. In retrospect, it strikes me that I was laughing not so much out of appreciation for his sense of humor but more out of my own personal sense of relief at having realized that John Rubino was my friend.

I certainly had my doubts when I first met him. On that auspicious occasion, about a month prior to the bathroom caper, I was working the day watch out of Hang Flight Systems. It was a slow day as days go, a day that implored me to commence thinking about where my next plate of beans would be coming from. I was studiously avoiding that surly question — waving my fingers in front of my face and otherwise dabbling in catatonia — when the man I would later come to know as Captain Cool Shoes strolled into the shop.

Thirty seconds into our conversation I realized that my standard "We're the greatest — Come on down — Sign up with us" rap wasn't gonna get it with this guy. I was in for a serious game of "Solma-Yahbut" which went something like this:

Shoes: Solma licensed jet airplane pilot!

Me: Yahbut that don't mean you got any advantage over the next guy when it comes to flying hang divers!

Shoes: Yahbut I can drive sailplanes and I useta fly hang gliders back in the OLD days when you were just a pup.

Me: SoIma a big stinking mozarella cheese THESE days and I'm tellin' ya it ain't like it was. Ya kinda gotta start over.

Shoes: Yahbut maybe yer not givin' me enough credit. No offense but I don't think yer all that bright.

Me: SoIma guy who can take constructive criticism from arrogant types like yerself (no offense) so why don't YOU tell ME how I can get some of yer money, tune you into the new gliders, and make us BOTH happy?

Shoes: One day at a time, son, one day at a time.

Me: Great! See ya Sunday!

Shoes: Did I agree to that?

Me: Would I lie to someone with your vast experience and aviation background?

Shoes: No, I guess not. See ya Sunday.

Fortunately, over the course of the next few weeks me 'n Shoes develop a grudging respect for one another. I learn that he is indeed a pretty exceptional aviator and he learns that I'm not blowin' smoke when I say that flying a modern glider is a tad different from flying his old Seagull III. Consequently, I stop trying to jam him into a convenient "student pidgeonhole" and he abandons his "I know better" stance. Thus the way is cleared for us to become friends.

You already know how John P.'s bathroom statement got the ball rolling. Now you get to hear how he came to bear the nickname "Captain Cool Shoes."

John shows up at the shop on a Monday after a Sunday which had seen him make a lot of progress towards getting wired into his new used glider. He was so stoked about things coming together that he'd gone out and bought a pair of super duper, hi-tech, ultralite, running/hiking shoes which were sure to guarantee exceptionally crisp launches. He was so stoked by the shoes that he decided to drop by with a six pack to show them off (to revel in the breakthrough that they symbolized). Fortunately, the instant I see the shoes and pick up on how he feels about them, I have the good sense to shriek out: "That's it!! I been searchin' all around for somethin' cool to call you!! From now on I'm gonna call you 'Cool Shoes'!!!"

A suddenly stunned John P. Rubino freezes in mid revel and, in a voice choked with mock hurt and seriousness, exclaims: "But ERRRIKK, I always wanted a FANCY nickname that would make people look UP to me----like----like----like 'THE CAPTAIN' or somethin'!"

"OK, OK!! 'CAPTAIN Cool Shoes' it is — but don't ever let me hear no guff about me not showin' you no respect!!" I shoot back as we both fall down laughing.

ALFALFA

Ya'll already met John Shook in article 17. His sensitive and profound, not to mention comical, portrayal of an X/C driver for me, Spanky, and Buckwheat won him critical acclaim from around the world. Certainly the U.S. Well, at LEAST Texas, Arizona, and Colorado. How about Dallas, Arivaca, and Denver? WOULD YOU BELIEVE parts of those cities?? (Oh, never mind.)

Anyway, if you recall, I described John then as a long tall Texan whom I considered one of my best students "... despite the fact that he is essentially a human analogy to a Gatling Gun and 'wuffo' questions are his bullets."

Just to bring you up to date, John, grinnin', drawlin', and DEMANDIN' to know everything under the sun, completes his training with us. He goes back home to Colorado for a spell, then appears from time to time in parts of California, Arizona, and Texas where he continues to ask questions in that soft drawl of his, and continues his development as a pilot.

For my part, I come to count on seeing Alfalfa and his brother Tom every six months or so when they pop up in my neck of the woods to swap tall tales and trade their beaver pelts for various sorts of hang gliding gear. Last time around the tales are of towing and the enormous potential it holds for flatlanders and other folks without accessible mountain launch points.

FRIENDS VS. THE LAST GUARANTEE

Captain Cool Shoes and Alfalfa. Over a period of months and years they become "Valued friends — Sharers of grins." Beyond that, as far as I know, the only thing they have in common is "The last guarantee."

The last guarantee for owners of hang gliding establishments, for members of the hang gliding community, is this: Sooner or later you're gonna lose some friends.

John Rubino and John Shook both died tragically in May of 1984.

The Captain, who loved all forms of aviation, went in on a two place ultralight while exploring that realm of flight with another licensed pilot. Details of the accident are unknown at this time. An FAA investigation is in progress. The newspaper, as newspapers do, reported that the aircraft "... plunged and crashed, but did not burn" whatever that means.

John Shook died as a result of a towing accident out near Tucson. Rumor has it that he hooked into the tow line but not the glider, released the tow line at 300' AGL, and fell to his death while going for his chute. Brother Tom witnessed the whole thing and was treated for shock on the scene. An accident report is being prepared by Tom whose grief is, understandably, immense.

THE VORTEX

In the vortex of confusion, anger, sadness, regret, and grief that I experienced following news of John Rubino's death I damned ultralights for their abysmal safety record, Cool Shoes for deserting me, and fate for taking such an exceptional person — a person whose friendship had become important to me — a person I wanted to know better.

As it was I did the best I could and found out more about him by attending the memorial service in his honor. I found out there that I was right about Shoes — he was an exceptional dude, the kind who leaves a lasting, warm impression on those whose lives he touches. I think about him a lot and miss him terribly already.

THE BLACK CLOUD

The black cloud was just lifting when, on a R&R journey to Mingus Mountain, Arizona, I learned that John Shook had died a week before Rubino's accident. That was not long ago and, except for an immediate fleeting (currently nagging) desire to get as far away from this stinking avocation as humanly possible, I have been unable to grieve the loss of the friend I knew as Alfalfa. I suspect that it will have to wait until the next time I see Tom.

In the meantime, the hang gliding instructor inside me is screaming to sound the following warning: As promising as the new towing technology seems to be, if you are newly engaged in towing activities at this time, you should consider yourself part of a TEST GROUP. You are experimenting with a launch technique that is, AT BEST, SLIGHTLY MORE DANGEROUS than foot launch because you are relying on more things (people, equipment) that can go wrong. Think about it.

FRIENDS

Getting back to the point at hand, I have one final thought to express before concluding this most difficult installment of The Right Stuff. For some reason, the feelings I experienced as a result of losing two friends compelled me to write about them, to share with you what I liked best about them. Looking back at what I've written, it's apparent to me that what I liked most about John and John were their unique senses of humor, their respective ways of extracting enjoyment from this deal called life. John Rubino, the sly and uproarious. John Shook, the quietly determined practitioner of "Texas Droll." Good people. Good friends.

And it's clear to me now why I felt compelled to share them with you.

Listen:

"Grief, like grins
Should be shared with yo' frens'"

So, like-----uhhhhhhh-----Thanks for being there — know what I mean?

25. The Test

You know all the stuff you've been reading about in these articles — takeoff technique, landing technique, exploring your glider's speed range, Intermediate Syndrome, what a "wuffo" is, etc.? Well, when these articles appeared in <u>Hang Gliding</u> magazine, I gave the readers the opportunity to take a test to see how much they remembered. That's right — TEST!

What follows are the correct answers for the test questions. I've also included what I considered the funniest answers from the comedians who responded.

FILL IN THE BLANKS

1. The two most critical aspects of hang glider flight are **launch** and **landing** because they occur slightly above stall speed and close to the ground.

   Shecky Green said **having fun** and **staying safe.**

2. With your hands off the control bar your glider will fly at **trim** speed which for most gliders is somewhere between **minimum sink** speed and **best glide** speed.

   Henny Youngman said **at the side of the hill** and **terminal velocity.**

3. You are flying along in your glider and you notice that the glider is not responding to your attempts to turn it. You feel no air on your face and it's very quiet. You realize you are **stalled** and you correct the situation by **pulling in on the control bar.**

   Slappy White said **on the ground** and **taking off.**

4. From completion of your final approach turn to the time you enter ground effect (several feet from the ground) you should fly at **best glide** speed or even faster if conditions are strong.

The mad punster responded **a fast speed.**

5. Some of the sources of information for Novice pilots (and all other pilots for that matter) are: **other pilots, schools, books and mags, clubs, USHGA Pilot Proficiency Rating System, Annual Accident Review.**

The unknown comic replied **411, 1-555-1212, mom,** and **dad.**

6. To qualify for a Novice rating a pilot must, among other things, be able to demonstrate three consecutive landings within **100** feet of a target. These landings must be: **safe and smooth, on feet,** and **into the wind.**

Bob Hope said **both, down wind, silly looking,** and **right side up.**

7. A requirement for all USHGA ratings (Beginner through Advanced) is that for each flight the pilot demonstrates a method for establishing that he or she is **hooked in** just prior to **launch.**

Rodney Dangerfield opted for **not asleep, landing.**

8. Shortly after completing your final approach turn you encounter a thermal. Generally speaking the best thing to do is **pull in to speed up.** If you **push out and slow down** you risk turbulence induced loss of control.

Flip Wilson went with **not to land** and **go home.**

DEFINITIONS

1. Hang Glider

The correct definition is: **An ultra light weight, ultra low speed airfoil capable of being foot launched and landed.**

Richard Pryor wrote: **Something between drugs and sex.** Franken and Davis preferred: **Some sheets with wire and poles.**

2. Intermediate Syndrome

The correct definition is: **The tendency of a relatively inexperienced pilot to become so overwhelmed by the exhilaration of flight that he or she forgets or ignores his or her own limitations and those of his equipment.**

Phyllis Diller believed it was: **Problems with dates.**

3. Wuffo

The correct definition is: **A term generally used to describe non-pilots who ask dumb questions about hang gliding. More accurately it is any pilot who is willing to learn from his mistakes.**

Bill Cosby saw it as: **The sound a dog makes when you land in his backyard uninvited.**

4. Wind Gradient

The correct definition is: **The tendency of the velocity of a breeze to diminish as the surface of a solid is approached.**

Dan Akroyd insisted it was: **A system for evaluating conditions: Downwind = F, Soarable = A.**

5. Best Glide

The correct definition is: **The airspeed at which the glider has the best (most efficient) lift to drag ratio.**

Rich Romero says, and I agree: **Yosemite.**

6. Stall

The correct definition is: **A turbulent separation of the airflow over the wing caused by an excessively high angle of attack. Normally associated (in unaccelerated flight) with the glider's lowest usable speed, stall results in loss of lift, increase in drag, and usually in a profound loss of control.**

Cheech and Chong hold that it is: **A place to relieve yourself after six hours in the air.**

7. Minimum Sink

The correct definition is: **The airspeed at which a glider's rate of descent is the lowest.**

Don Rickles claims it is: **The least money you can sink into the latest hot kite on the market.** (You hockey puck.)

8. Ground Effect

The correct definition is: **Increased performance (L/D) of a hang glider within a wing span of the ground due to the ground blocking the extension of wingtip vortices which reduces induced drag.**

George Burns says: **Bad mood due to insufficient air time.**

MULTIPLE CHOICE

1. The question was ...

Which of the following is NOT an axis of rotation for a hang glider?

a) pitch
b) yaw
c) prone
d) roll

Pitch, yaw, and roll are axes of rotation for hang gliders. **Prone** is not.

2. The question was ...

Landing is in one sense more demanding than takeoff because:

a) You must concentrate totally.
b) You must control your angle of attack precisely.
c) You can pick the exact moment you want to launch whereas you can't pick the exact moment you want to land.

The correct answer is c: **You can pick the exact moment you want to launch whereas you can't pick the exact moment you want to land.** Total concentration and precise control of angle of attack are of equal (and utmost) importance in both situations.

3. The question was ...

Hang gliding is:

a) Absolute lunacy.
b) Inherently dangerous.
c) Safe and rewarding.
d) Any of the above, depending on how you go about it.

Hang gliding is not necessarily a) absolute lunacy, b) inherently dangerous, or c) safe and rewarding. It is **any of the above, depending on how you go about it.**

ESSAY:

Lastly, the readers were asked to write an essay on the ever-burning question (and one often asked by woofos) ...

You are flying along in your hand glider and all of a sudden (just before your arms get tired) THE WIND STOPS! Quick!! What do you do?

The responses to this question were many and varied but most included some variation of "Pull in on the control bar to regain airspeed because the sudden stopping of the wind has put you in a stalled condition."

Some folks felt that the best thing to do would be to go in quickly and land. This is a reasonable response if the rationale behind it is, "Hey, the wind suddenly stopping like that means conditions are too gusty for a sane man to fly in." It is an unreasonable response if the rationale is, "Hey, these here hang gliders are powered by the wind so if it stops, I'm out of power so I'd better land."

Gliders, of course, are powered by gravity, not the wind.

Some responses were based on the assumption that gliders are powered by lift (ridge and/or thermal) and that the wind stopping means no more lift so "I'm out of power and I'd better land."

Once again, gliders are powered by gravity. Gravity causes a glider to move constantly downward through the air. If a thermal is going up at 800 fpm, a glider in it is only going away from the ground at 600 fpm because gravity causes it to go down through the air in the thermal at 200 fpm (minimum sink).

Then, of course, we had the usual comedian responses, such as: "change underwear, go blind, scream bloody murder, review your priorities", etc. I'm beginning to think that HUMOR, not gravity, powers hang gliders.

Actually, the correct answer is:

Relax, the glider will take care of itself.

Yes, folks, the correct answer to the question "What do you DO when the wind stops?" is: Nothing.

The only assumption on which the "nothing" response is based is that the pilot is already flying at an airspeed appropriate to the conditions that exist just before the wind stops. Remember that heavier conditions call for faster flying speeds so that if you are flying in moderately strong conditions you should be cruising at best glide speed.

GRADING THE TEST

How can you to grade a test that has the answers given with the questions? Easy. Your grade is determined by what you were saying to yourself while "taking" the test.

Let's say you were rolling along smugly chortling to yourself: "I know this!" "This stuff's easy!" or "Any fool could answer these dumb questions!" Give yourself an **A**! You done good!

Let's say one or two of the questions made you think: "Hmmmmm — I didn't know that" or "Well goodness me, imagine that." Give yourself a **B**. You still done good.

Let's say several (more than two, less than five) of the questions made you ask yourself: "Did I miss something around here or what?" Give yourself a **C**. You done OK.

Now, let's say that most or all of the time you were slappin' your forehead and muttering: "Huh?" or "Whu?" Or worse, let's say your eyes glazed over half way through and you found your little finger digging at the wax in your ear. Give yourself a **D** or an **F**, it don't matter which. You done bad and you shouldn't oughta get within a hundred yards of no hang gliders until you know more about how and why they work.

26. Resolutions, Revelations, Inspirations, and a Checklist or Two

The whole point of this piece, of course, is for all of us to swear up and down that we'll do a whole bunch of smart, reasonable things to keep us safe as we go about pursuing the truth and beauty of flying hang gliders.

RESOLUTIONS

Let's talk always. I will always:

1. Remember that hang gliding is a high risk, high reward endeavor.

2. Realize that the only way I can minimize the risks and maximize the rewards is to approach hang gliding with an enormous amount of responsibility and self-discipline.

3. Be aware of and utilize all sources of information available to me, including written material, schools, clubs, and (selectively) more experienced pilots.

4. Be aware of the USHGA Pilot Proficiency Rating System and utilize it as a framework for scheduling and implementing new learning experiences.

5. Recognize that launching and landing are the two most critical aspects of hang glider flight since both occur close to the cold, hard ground at airspeeds very near stall.

6. Work at perfecting my launch and landing technique.

7. Be aware of what my glider feels, sounds, looks, and smells like at airspeeds ranging from stall to minimum sink to best glide to fast to real fast.

8. Recognize the limits of my knowledge and experience so that I don't fall prey to Intermediate Syndrome.

9. Make sure that the glider I fly is airworthy in regard to design (HGMA certified) and construction as well as state of repair and tune. Make sure that I have read and understood the owner's manual that comes with my glider.

10. Make sure that all other equipment I use (harness, carabiners, helmets, parachutes) is properly designed, constructed, and maintained according to manufacturers' recommendations.

11. Pre-flight check my glider before flying.

12. Do a hang check to confirm hook-in JUST PRIOR to launch.

Let's talk never. I will never:

1. Forget that hang gliding is a high risk, high reward endeavor.

2. Survive if I go about hang gliding in a careless or neglectful way.

3. Allow myself to get in over my head out of ignorance or self-imposed isolation from the rest of the hang gliding community.

4. Brazenly "go for it" when my skill level dictates "sit on it" just because conditions are "really happenin' man."

5. View launching and landing as kid stuff not worthy of consideration by a jaded three month expert such as myself.

6. Work at perfecting my "slopover" aerobatic maneuvers just because my girlfriend (or boyfriend) loves it when I scream.

7. Fly blindfolded, or with earplugs, or with my hands tied behind my back.

8. Hook in and take off in a 30-degree cross wind gusting from 15 to 45 mph just because Ace McHotshot is somehow managing to avoid tumbling his Deathwing 500 a thousand feet over takeoff.

9. Buy a "Flyspeck" from someone named Lefty who says the 45-degree downward bend in the left leading edge "takes care of a slight right turn" in this all-but-certified (except for load testing and filming) state of the art hang glider.

10. Fly without a helmet or parachute or in a harness fabricated from burlap and baling twine by "Buy-lo Accessories, Inc."

11. Forget to pre-flight.

12. Forget to hook in.

REVELATIONS AND INSPIRATIONS

Flying hang gliders is fun!
Flying hang gliders is NOT INHERENTLY SAFE.
Flying hang gliders CAN BE MADE SAFE by the way you go about it.
Your own fate is in your own hands.

A CHECKLIST OR TWO

Welcome each new year by making sure all your equipment is in good shape.

Glider. If you've had your glider for a year or more it is a good idea to do or have done a thorough inspection.

1. Remove the sail from the frame.

2. Inspect all frame components for dents, gouges, bends, signs of fatigue or corrosion. Pull the end caps and look inside.

3. Inspect all wires for frays, kinks, thimble elongation or deformation. Be especially picky about your side flying wires.

4. Check all bolts and fittings for bends or signs of wear.

5. Inspect the sail.

6. Replace parts as necessary.

7. Replace all nyloc nuts you've removed during disassembly.

8. Replace hang strap even if it looks perfect.

9. Do a thorough inspection following any crash.

Equipment.

1. Inspect harness: all support straps, leg straps, stitching, main body, etc. Look for signs of wear, frays, cuts, and material defects. Some manufacturers recommend changing main support straps (usually those nearest hips) annually. This will cost you $10-20.

2. Inspect carabiner. Locking gate type is best.

3. Inspect helmet shell and liner. Replace if cracked, or moldy, or filled with bugs.

4. Replace parachute after practice deployment and thorough inspection of canopy, gore lines, and bridle by qualified rigger. Repack is generally recommended every six months.

SUMMARY

Make sure all the stuff you buy and use is good stuff.
Keep your stuff in good shape.
Always do things right.
Never do things wrong.
Have fun.
Be safe.

Index